TORONTO AND THE CAMERA SERIES

MIKE FILEY & VICTOR RUSSELL

FROM HORSE POWER
TO HORSEPOWER

TORONTO: 1890–1930

For Yarmila & Donna

And with thanks to

Staff of the City of Toronto Archives

Staff of the Toronto Sun Library

Charles Abel Photo Finishing and Irene

Pat Curran, CAA

Ted Wickson, Toronto Transit Commission

Nancy Hurn, Metro Toronto Archives

Bruce Humphrey, Humphrey Funeral Home

TORONTO AND THE CAMERA SERIES

MIKE FILEY & VICTOR RUSSELL

FROM HORSE POWER TO HORSEPOWER

TORONTO: 1890–1930

Dundurn Press
Toronto & Oxford

Design: Andy Tong
Editor: Judith Turnbull
Printed and bound in Canada by WEBCOM, Scarborough, Ontario

The publisher wishes to acknowledge the generous assistance and ongoing support of **The Canada Council**, **The Book Publishing Industry Development Program** of the **Department of Communications, The Ontario Arts Council, The Ontario Publishing Centre** of the **Ministry of Culture, Tourism and Recreation**, and **The Ontario Heritage Foundation**.
Care has been taken to trace the ownership of copyright material used in the text (including the illustrations). The author and publisher welcome any information enabling them to rectify any reference or credit in subsequent editions.

J. Kirk Howard, Publisher

Canadian Cataloguing in Publication Data

Filey, Mike, 1941–
            From Horse Power to Horsepower : Toronto, 1890–1930

(Toronto and the Camera)
ISBN 1-55002-200-8

1. Transportation – Ontario – Toronto – History.   2. Transportation – Ontario – Toronto – Pictorial works. I. Russell, Victor L. (Victor Loring), 1948–   .
II. Title.

HE311.C32T64   1993   388'.9713'541   C93-095353-3

Front cover photograph: St. Clair Avenue and Keele Street, c. 1925 (Mike Filey Collection)
Photo of Mike Filey (back cover): courtesy of the *Toronto Sun*
Photo of Victor Russell (back cover): courtesy of Records and Archives Division

We thank the Ford Motor Company of Canada and General Motors of Canada for permission to reproduce the Ford and Chevrolet ads that appear in this book.

Dundurn Press Limited	**Dundurn Distribution**	**Dundurn Press Limited**
2181 Queen Street East	73 Lime Walk	1823 Maryland Avenue
Suite 301	Headington, Oxford	P.O. Box 1000
Toronto, Canada	England	Niagara Falls, N.Y.
M4E 1E5	0X3 7AD	U.S.A. 14302-1000

Contents

Prologue in Pictures

The six photographs in this section, which were taken by Frank W. Micklethwaite and date from circa 1890, show the city streets just before the onslaught of motorized vehicles – not an auto or electric streetcar in sight, yet. The reader is challenged to identify the location of each photo. Stumped? The locations are listed on the last page of the book.

4

Introduction

From the late 1890s to 1930, the city of Toronto underwent more change than at any period in its history. In a little more than three decades, the city was transformed from a moderately successful Victorian city to a 20th-century industrial urban centre. Throughout this period, the population grew unrelentingly, the area of the city expanded significantly (primarily through annexation of neighbouring municipalities), and the industrial sector of the city's economy established itself as pre-eminent.

As historian Jesse E. Middleton noted in 1923, "Approaching the last decade of the Nineteenth Century, Toronto found itself no longer a compact little city, but a straggling big one, outgrowing its civic services as rapidly as a small boy outgrows his pantaloons" (*History of Toronto*, 1923).

Successive municipal councils worked desperately to keep pace. Important changes were made in city governance, such as the first election of a board of control in 1903. Then, in 1912, the corporation underwent a major reorganization, creating a departmental structure that it hoped could provide such basic municipal services as roads, sewers, water, public transportation, and police and fire protection. Vast sums of money were committed to modernizing the city, and total capital expenditures grew from $5.6 million in 1900 to $82.5 million in 1930.

One of the key factors prompting all of this was the advent of the motor vehicle. Urban historians have recently begun to re-evaluate the impact of motorized vehicles on the city, and there is a growing consensus that in the first three decades of this century the car, together with its cousins, the truck, the bus, and the electric streetcar, was the single most important factor in transforming the city from a 19th-century town to a 20th-century metropolis. Streets were paved, bridges were built, and traffic lights and signs were installed to organize the growing chaos. At the same time, car dealers and service centres became a regular feature of the streetscape, parking lots were opened, and Toronto experienced its first traffic jam. In response, local and provincial governments were forced to introduce a myriad of regulations, covering everything from licensing to speed limits. Public transportation was motorized, rationalized, and taken over by the municipality during this period and, with the addition of buses, began to play an important role in the movement of a burgeoning work force.

This book contains historical photographs of the city during these years. The emphasis is on cars, trucks, streetcars, buses – all forms of the motorized vehicles that began to appear in increasing numbers on the streets of Toronto around the turn of the century. To some degree the book is a visual record of the various forms of transportation developed during the first 30 years of the 20th century. Ford's Model T, Indian and Henderson motorcycles, the Witt streetcar, the Cadillac delivery truck, firetrucks, and even street-cleaning vehicles are all predecessors of the thousands of machines we now take for granted in our daily lives both at home and at work. However, when these vehicles appeared in public for the first time, they created excitement, if not wonder.

Torontonians, like everyone else, became obsessed with modern forms of transportation. Crowds would gather to catch a glimpse of one of the new machines; motor shows were organized (several a year); and government and industry moved quickly to acquire motorized versions of wagons and other equipment. In 1903 there were only 243 licensed vehicles in the province; by 1929 there were 527,936, one-quarter of them in Toronto.

During this same period, there were important changes in the role of photographers. No longer were they restricted to taking studio portraits. Following the turn of the century, photographers took pictures for reproduction in the daily newspapers, they documented public works, and they recorded the usual and the unusual. The art was practised by amateur and professional alike. Fortunately, Toronto had its share of talented professional photographers throughout the late 19th and early 20th centuries, and it is no surprise that developments in transportation were often the subject of their work.

It is also fortunate that many of these photographs survive in the collections of the City of Toronto Archives. Established in 1960, the City Archives have actively acquired the works of Toronto photographers. After more than 30 years of collecting, the archives now house more than 200 historical collections totalling more than one million images. The 19th-century works of Armstrong, Beere and Hime, Octavius Thompson, Josiah Bruce, Frank Micklethwaite, Alexander Galbraith, and Notman Studios are represented. And the 20th-century collections are dominated by the works of the city's official photographer Arthur Goss, freelance photo-journalist William James, and Toronto *Globe* staff photographer John Boyd.

This book is a thematic presentation of the work of these fine photographers. While its subject – transportation developments – is one that dominated the period when these photographers were active, other themes could just as easily have been chosen to demonstrate the quality of their work. William James's uncanny knack for capturing the moment, Arthur Goss's technical skills, and John Boyd's talent as a photo-journalist are evident in the photographs collected here. Together these pictures illustrate the research and aesthetic value of archival photos, but at the same time, they offer us a glimpse of a truly dynamic period in our city's history.

Except for those otherwise identified, all photographs reproduced here are from the City of Toronto Archives.

The Photographers

WILLIAM JAMES (1866–1948)

The James prints featured in the following pages are but a representative sampling of the 6,000 images included in the James Collection. Acquired by the City of Toronto Archives in 1976, this collection of historical photographs is a unique pictorial record of life in Toronto from 1907 through 1936.

Noted for his technical expertise and sense of composition, William James was one of the first photographers to recognize the value and potential impact of unposed, human-interest photos. This immediacy and informality resulted in candid, often humorous, and sometimes dramatic documentary photographs. In his capacity as a freelance news photographer, James recorded the entire social and political spectrum of life in Toronto. The majority of the images included in this book depict Toronto going about its daily business, oblivious to the camera.

Born in 1866 in Walsall, England, and one of eight children in a working-class family, James immigrated to Canada in 1906 at the age of 40. For the next three years, he drifted through a variety of jobs, including insurance salesman, manager of the National Club, and telegraph office sales representative. Throughout this period he continued to devote all of his leisure hours to honing his photographic skills. By 1909 he was ready to make his living from his art.

Following some early lean years when he specialized in stereographs (double-mounted photographs that appear three-dimensional when seen through a special viewer), James found success in news and commercial photography. He did not, however, work on an assignment basis for the newspapers. He chose his own subjects, spending the daylight hours photographing people, places, and events of interest. In the evening he would hurriedly develop and print the day's output and then make the rounds of the seven or eight daily and weekly newspapers printed in the city at that time, selling his best efforts at the going rate of $2 per print.

The competitive nature of the Toronto newspaper scene, coupled with the fact that staff photographers were unheard of at the time, provided a lucrative market for James's prolific creations. His work appeared in leading publications of the day – *Toronto World, Mayfair, Canadian Horseman, Hunting in Canada,* and *Chatelaine.* His best customer, however, was the *Toronto Daily Star.* He developed a working relationship with this paper that was destined to span two generations.

James was the founding president of the Canadian Photographers Association. He was also the first photographer in Canada to take aerial movies from the open cockpit of a biplane – his accomplishment being over Toronto in 1916. While his experience in moving pictures proved to be financially disastrous, the quality of his work was never in question. Much of the movie film taken by James during the First World War is now preserved in the National Archives of Canada in Ottawa.

James was as innovative in the darkroom as he was behind the camera. A pioneer in photographic processing, he invented a special type of developer that reduced grain, and he worked with telephoto lenses, indoor time exposures, and infra-red film. James also designed and built his own cameras. Oddly, he found the switch from glass to film negatives difficult and he used British-made photographic materials exclusively. His career took him from the old wet-plate process, through glass negatives, to cut film, to roll film. For 40 years James documented life in Toronto, until his death in 1948.

JOHN H. BOYD (1898–1971)

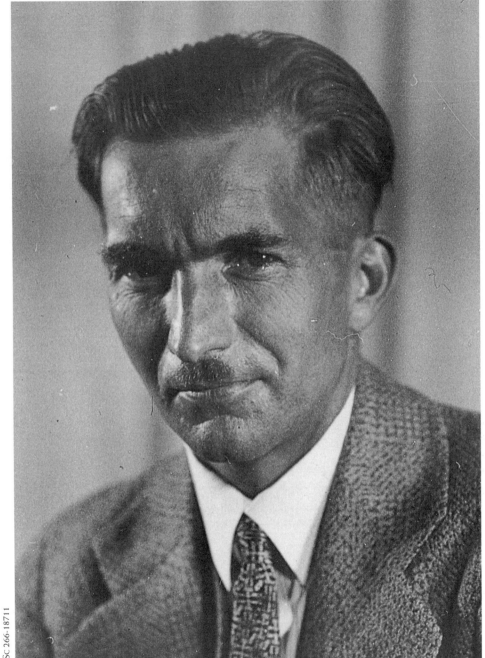

John Harold Boyd, the son of John and Alice Boyd, was born in Toronto on January 11, 1898. His father, John Sr., an employee first of the Grand Trunk Railway and then, until his retirement, of the Canadian National Railways, was a well-respected amateur photographer whose photographic experimentation extended to the construction of his own cameras, the design of several timing guides for exposures, and the production of unique double exposures. John Jr. received his early training in photography while working at his father's side.

In 1921, at the age of 23, Boyd began work at the *Globe* as a freelance photographer. In 1922 he was hired as the newspaper's first and only staff photographer. He remained with the *Globe* after its amalgamation with the *Mail and Empire* in 1936, continuing in the position of chief photographer until his retirement in February 1963.

John Boyd was a founding member of the Commercial and Press Photographers' Association of Canada (CAPPAC), which was organized in 1947 and incorporated in 1948 as a national association of Canadian professional photographers. Boyd served as its first president for two successive terms. Subsequently, he continued to participate in the areas of membership, publication, judging, and speaking engagements. In 1962 CAPPAC formally changed its name to the Professional Photographers of Canada.

Boyd is often remembered for being the first to use a camera smaller than the popular 5″ x 7″ press graphlex. His use of a

$3^{1}/4'' \times 4^{1}/4''$ graphlex became his long-lasting trademark. He also gained recognition for transmitting the first Canadian wire-photo during his coverage of a provincial by-election in East Hastings in 1936. Described by his colleagues as a colourful character, Boyd was the butt of many jokes relating to the inventive way he restyled his cameras, giving them a rather "distinct appearance."

Boyd's work is characterized by its painstaking attention to detail. His meticulous approach is best illustrated by his scrupu-lously detailed system for documenting his assignments. The logbooks that accompany the Globe and Mail Collection of negatives were maintained by Boyd, who recorded the number, subject, and date of every negative. The photo-negatives, totalling more than 100,000, and the logbooks were donated to the City of Toronto Archives by the *Globe and Mail*.

Arthur S. Goss (1881–1940)

William Arthur Scott Goss was born on March 4, 1881, in London, Ontario. In 1883 the family moved to Toronto, where John Goss was involved in several journalistic enterprises. Arthur Goss entered Rose Avenue Public School in 1889 but was withdrawn following his father's death in 1891. At age 11, he was employed by the City of Toronto as an office boy in the City Engineer's Office. He was to remain an employee of this department his entire life.

In April 1904 Goss joined the Toronto Camera Club, an organization of dedicated non-professionals that had formed in Toronto in 1891. Goss immediately took an active role in the club and served as vice-president in 1905. That same year he joined with several club members to form the Studio Club, modelled on the British "Linked Ring." Linked Ring's advocacy of pictorial photography was based on a desire to explore the "potentialities of photography as a medium of artistic expression" and to provide international exhibitions. Goss and the members of the Studio Club enjoyed instant success. As early as 1906 their activities received favourable notices both at home and abroad. Goss's involvement in the Toronto Camera Club and its exhibitions was sporadic after 1915. The few surviving examples of his work as a pictorialist are preserved in the City Archives along with the more than 25,000 images he created as city photographer.

The City Engineer's Office staff had begun to take photographs on a limited scale in 1899. This sort of documentation was soon flourishing, and from 1911 to 1940 Goss was employed by the Department of Public Works' Photography and Blue Printing Section, where he systematically recorded a vast range of municipal activities. In sharp contrast to the soft-lens portraits and artistic landscapes of the pictorialist style, Goss's photographic record of Toronto is characterized by striking realism.

The survival in the City Archives of most of Goss's work as Toronto's official photographer has led to his recognition as one of the most important documentary photographers working in Canada in the early 20th century. The more than 30,000 photographs produced by the Photography and Blue Printing Section were taken for specific administrative purposes – to illustrate a report, accompany a lecture, or monitor the progress of a construction project. Most of these pictures document the daily operations of the Works Department – the building of bridges, the laying of street railway tracks, the widening of streets.

Goss also worked on assignment for other departments, producing, for example, over 2,000 pictures tracing parks development between 1912 and 1945, a complete record of a home renovation program operated by the city during the Depression, and documentation of the concerns and activities of the Department of Public Health from 1911 to 1940. The photographs created by Goss for the Health Department are among the most significant in the collection. They were commissioned by reform-minded Dr. Charles Hastings, Toronto's medical officer of health.

The creation of this outstanding civic record ended with Goss's death in 1940.

FRANK W. MICKLETHWAITE (1849–1925)

Frank Micklethwaite was born in England, though the family later moved to Ireland. The son of a photographer, Micklethwaite had a chance to learn his profession, possibly as an apprentice, before emigrating to Canada around 1875. After a brief stint as a proofreader at the *Mail* newspaper in Toronto, he opened his commercial photography studio at his home on Queen Street West, in 1878. For the next 30 years, Micklethwaite operated a studio at various locations around the city, finally settling his business at 243 Yonge Street.

Micklethwaite's growing reputation and financial stability improved steadily, and numerous assignments came his way. Between 1891 and 1898, for example, he was commissioned by the City of Toronto to document a number of public works projects. These photographs, for which Micklethwaite was paid a total of $310, record major reconstruction of the city's water and sewage systems, street-grading projects, and bridge improvements. Respected by his peers, Micklethwaite was asked in 1893 to participate in the judging of the second annual Toronto Camera Club exhibition.

In 1895 Micklethwaite's eldest son, John, joined the business, an event repeated in 1898 and again in 1899, when sons Percy and Fred became active partners. The business continued to produce quality images that document many Toronto landmarks, street views, and prominent social gatherings.

Micklethwaite also operated a seasonal studio at Port

Sandfield in the Muskoka Lakes. In failing health towards the end of his life, Micklethwaite increasingly entrusted the operation of the studio to his sons, and on his death in 1925, Fred assumed the business. In turn, Fred's son, Jack Micklethwaite, was active in photography until the 1970s, almost completing the century since Frank had opened on Queen Street.

The City Archives has many fine works produced by the Micklethwaites, both from the City Engineer's Office collection and from a collection acquired from Jack, containing photos taken by various members of the family.

From Horse Power to Horsepower

Motor vehicles first appeared on Toronto streets as a kind of novelty, near the end of the 19th century. Most were owned and operated by inventors or hobbyists, and while they attracted a great deal of attention, these early vehicles were not available to the public.

Within a few short years all this changed. The technology improved dramatically, and the number of manufacturers of motor vehicles increased, as did the number of machines. From the beginning, the industry adopted the "motor show" as a means of introducing its products to the public. By the early 20th century, formal exhibits were organized for virtually every type of vehicle. At first, cars, trucks, motorboats, and working vehicles were exhibited together, but gradually, separate shows were held for different types of vehicles.

Similarly, innovations in mass transit, such as streetcars, buses, and trains, were often exhibited to a fascinated public, usually at the annual Canadian National Exhibition (CNE).

Frederick Barnard Fetherstonhaugh was a well-known Toronto patent attorney who, in 1893, contracted with British-born electrician William Still and the Dixon Carriage works on Bay Street to build Canada's first electric car. His interest in the patent business and the new inventions they spawned no doubt contributed to his interest in the development of automobiles. While the Dixon-built carriages incorporated many modern features, such as a folding top, electric lights, and tires with pneumatic inner tubes, it was really the source of motive power that made this vehicle unique. The 12-cell storage battery, designed by Still, fed electric current to a four-horsepower motor, resulting in approximately one full hour's driving time at 24 km/h.

The owner was able to recharge the car's battery by simply hooking up and "stepping down" the power from the overhead wires of the Sunnyside to Long Branch radial streetcar line, which ran along Lakeshore Road in front of Fetherstonhaugh's suburban Mimico residence.

When first demonstrated at the 1893 CNE, the little vehicle carried willing passengers around a small track in front of the old grandstand. The vehicle provided its owner with reliable and inexpensive transportation around town for about 15 years and was frequently on display at the CNE.

The famous Fetherstonhaugh electric car (right) on display in the CNE's Transportation Building, 1912.

Wm. James, SC 244-56

Motor show at the University Avenue Armories, 1912. The manufacturers displaying both cars and trucks at this show included Packard, Reo, Ford, Cadillac, and, under the T. Eaton Company banner, Lozier, Chalmers, Waverly, and Saurer.

Wm. James, SC 244-51a

The first motor show in North America was held at Madison Square Gardens in New York City in 1900. Soon after, Toronto dealers were advertising their versions of the "motor show," but these simply featured the models they had for sale in their own showrooms. It wasn't until March 1906 that Toronto's first motor show as we now know it opened to a curious public, who gladly paid the 25-cent admission fee to view the $400,000 worth of automobiles, motorboats, marine engines, and accessories, all neatly arranged on the two curling rink surfaces at the Granite Club on Church Street. A few days later, a second show, described as "the real big automobile show," was featured in the Mutual Street Rink (later known as the Arena and, just prior to its demolition a few years ago, as the Terrace). This event featured English and French autos such as the Napier, Argyle, Minerva, Triumph, Panhard, Daimler, and De Dion. Other shows were held at the University Avenue Armories and, by 1909, at the newly constructed Transportation Building at the Canadian National Exhibition Grounds.

In February 1929 a special edition of the National Auto Show was held in the new addition at Simpson's department store, at the northeast corner of Bay and Richmond streets. Cars for this exhibit were delivered to the Richmond Street side of Simpson's, carefully hoisted, by crane and block and tackle, up the outside of the building, man-handled through several large windows, and placed on display on the building's top four floors. The luxury automobiles had a place of honour on the eighth floor and its mezzanine. The cars on display at this event included the Chandler, Black Hawk, DeSoto, Jordan, LaSalle, Packard, Roosevelt, Stutz, and Whippet. The familiar Ford, Lincoln,

A Chalmers 36 in the Transportation Building, CNE, 1912.
Mike Filey Collection

Pontiac, Oldsmobile, Dodge, and Chevrolet nameplates were also there.

In the fall of that same year, and in time for the 1929 edition of the CNE, the show moved to the new Automotive Building at the Exhibition Grounds, where motor shows remained a popular CNE feature for another 40 years.

The CNE's Transportation Building, which was erected in 1909, featured "aeroplanes" in the 1920s and 1930s. The structure was destroyed by fire in 1974.

Mike Filey Collection

In 1929, as part of the development of the eastern end of the Exhibition Grounds, a new Automotive Building was erected at a cost of $1 million. It was designed by Toronto architect Douglas Kertland, and actual construction began on April 10, 1929. On August 26 ("Highways and Automotive Day"), a mere 138 days after work started, the new building was officially opened by Ontario premier Howard Ferguson and Toronto mayor Sam McBride. The latter described the structure as the "greatest automotive building in the world." McBride went on:

"It is truly a Canadian building; architect, contractors, materials and labour were all Canadian."

Exhibitors in the building that first year were General Motors, Ford, Chrysler, Dominion, Studebaker, Reo, Stewart, Fruehauf, International, Willys-Overland, Pierce Arrow, Nash, Durant, Stutz, Auburn, Hupmobile, and Packard.

The Motor Show at the Automotive Building was a feature attraction at the CNE until 1967.

The Automotive Building, CNE, seen from Boulevard Drive (now Lake Shore Boulevard) during the 1930 Exhibition.

Mike Filey Collection

The cornerstone of the new Automotive Building was laid (in the pouring rain) by Mayor Sam McBride on June 12, 1929.

Mike Filey Collection

Soon after the first motorized vehicles began appearing on the city's streets, service centres and dealers' showrooms opened their doors. These service industry establishments were often modified carriage or blacksmith shops, converted bicycle dealers, or storefront operations scattered around the city. By 1930 these establishments had become a permanent feature of the urban landscape.

William Park's tire repair shop, 357 Parliament Street at Oak Street, c. 1935.
A. Goss, SC 231-592

In addition to dispensing Castrol lubricants and selling and repairing car and truck tires, William Park sold Shell gasoline from this pair of pumps located at the curb in front of his Parliament Street shop. The placement of gas pumps on the sidewalk was an acceptable feature of the city streetscape until the Toronto Board of Control ordered that no new licences for this type of installation be issued after August 23, 1929.

Imperial Oil Service Station, 88 Danforth Avenue., 1926.
Imperial Oil Archives

British American Oil service station, Avenue Road and Lowther Avenue, 1927.
Pringle and Booth Collection, SC 185-39

It wasn't long after the first motor cars began appearing on the city's streets that places where they could be looked after sprang up, often as minor modifications to long-time carriage or blacksmith shops.

At the time these photos were taken, two of the most prominent suppliers of automotive fuels and lubricants were Imperial Oil and British American Oil. In 1907 in Vancouver, Imperial, a company still very much in evidence around the city today, opened what might very well have been North America's first service station. A few years later, Imperial opened its first Toronto station, serving Premier brand gasoline, which in the spring of 1914 sold for 22.5 cents per gallon (5 cents a litre).

The price dropped over the next few months, to as low as 17 cents per gallon in the summer of 1915. With gasoline in short supply after the war owing to the tremendous increase in motor cars on the roads, the price began to rise. By the end of 1920 that same gallon of gasoline was selling for 45.5 cents. When the two photos reproduced here were taken, the price had begun to drop again, to 31.7 cents per gallon in 1926 and 27.8 cents the following year. The dealer mark-up remained almost constant over the entire period, at approximately 3.5 cents per gallon. Interestingly, both the 1926 and 1927 figures, though significantly less than that for 1920, now included a provincial government gasoline tax that had first been applied to road fuel in early 1925.

Another familiar sight in Toronto in the early years of the 20th century was service stations operated by the British American Oil Company. Established in 1906, B-A erected the country's third refinery on three acres of secluded land in Toronto's Ashbridge's Bay area. Here the company refined kerosene (used in great quantities for illuminating purposes) and lubricating oils, letting the almost worthless gasoline by-product drain into a nearby swamp. (B-A continued to operate a plant at the foot of Cherry Street until 1948, when operations were consolidated at the Clarkson Refinery. Clarkson had gone on stream in 1943 specifically to produce aviation gasoline for the war effort.)

As the years went by, gasoline became more and more in demand. In 1925, to meet the needs of the ever-increasing number of automobile drivers, the company opened its first Toronto service station at the corner of Bloor Street and Delaware Avenue. From this location, and from the many that would soon follow, B-A dispensed its popular Peerless gasoline, "the aristocrat of premium gasolines," and their regular grade British Motor.

In the mid-1950s B-A became part of the Gulf Oil empire, though the well-known name of British American and the company's products at the gas pumps, 88 and 98, didn't disappear until the takeover was complete in 1969. Sixteen years later the assets of Gulf Canada were acquired by Petro-Canada.

The Spanish influenza epidemic of 1918–19 killed nearly 2,000 Torontonians.

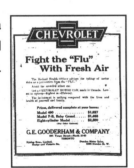

This automobile garage/Chevrolet dealership (facing page), rather grandiosely referred to as the Garrett Motor Company in the city directories of the day, was located on the west side of Yonge Street between Briar Hill and Albertus avenues in North Toronto.

The business was known as the Belmont Garage when it opened in 1917, the name no doubt selected as a result of the telephone number exchange assigned to Alexander Garrett's business by the Bell Telephone Company.

With the mobility of most Torontonians significantly increased following the end of the First World War, thanks in great measure to the production of inexpensive automobiles like

the Chevrolet pictured in this photograph (facing page), more and more citizens were moving into the suburban fringes that were developing around the city.

To serve this expanding population, the telephone company had to augment its system with new exchanges, thereby permitting the installation of more residential and business telephones.

The Belmont exchange grew out of the older North and Hillcrest exchanges that had been serving the north end of the community. As the number of phones in service approached the maximum capacity of these two exchanges, a new exchange became necessary. Belmont opened in 1916 in a building on Eglinton Avenue just east of Yonge, the site of the present Bell Canada structure.

In the foreground of the photograph, the tracks of the Metropolitan Division of the Toronto and York Radial Railway are visible. This high-speed electric interurban streetcar line, one of many that radiated out from the city, offered Torontonians another way to migrate away from the crowded city into the wide-open suburban areas.

The Metropolitan Division had as it origins a horsecar service (forerunner to the streetcar) that operated from the railway crossing south of St. Clair Avenue up Yonge Street, first to Eglinton Avenue (1885) and then, in stages, all the way north to the town of Newmarket (1899).

In 1904 the line came under the control of the Toronto and York Radial Railway Company, and over the next few years it continued to be extended northward, eventually reaching Jackson's Point (1907) and Sutton (1909).

On March 16, 1930, through-service from the city to the Lake Simcoe communities came to an end, though the more popular and subsidized Toronto–Richmond Hill section was reinstituted just four months later. Then, with the total abandonment of streetcars on north Yonge Street on October 10, 1948, that service too was shut down. All streetcar service on Yonge came to an end less than six years later when Toronto opened its first subway, on March 30, 1954.

Garrett's garage, 2574 Yonge Street, c. 1920.
A. Goss, SC 231-832

One of the flashiest cars to be seen on the streets of Toronto was the creation of George Pierce, an automaker from Buffalo, New York. The first Pierce Arrow rolled out of the factory in 1904, and before its demise in 1937, the legendary automobile had become one of the world's great "luxury" cars.

Toronto's Pierce Arrow dealer, H.E. Givan, engaged the prominent local architect William Sparling to design the showroom in which Pierce's elegant models could be displayed to their best advantage. The $90,000 structure opened in early 1930.

For a few years following the demise of the Pierce Arrow, the Givan dealership offered other makes for sale in its showroom, but it eventually abandoned the premises altogether in 1943. The space was then used for a variety of purposes until its purchase by the Canadian Broadcasting Corporation in 1954.

CBC-TV went on air in September 1952, and it was in this former auto showroom, CBC's Studio Four, that early Canadian television productions starring such personalities as Wayne and Shuster, Joan Fairfax, and Juliette originated. Early editions of "Front Page Challenge," "Flashback," and "The Tommy Hunter Show" were also produced at Studio Four.

Detail of decorative carving by artist Merle Foster on Yonge Street facade of the old Pierce Arrow showroom, 1993.
Mike Filey Collection

Pierce Arrow showroom, 1140 Yonge Street at Marlborough Avenue, c. 1930.
Pringle and Booth Collection, SC 185-37

The Willys-Overland Company, whose founder John North Willys began his career selling Pierce and Rambler automobiles in 1902, began building motor cars in its Toledo, Ohio, factory in 1907. In its first year, it built a total of 465 cars. By 1910 the company was turning out 18,200 cars annually. Five years later almost 92,000 cars rolled off its assembly line, making Willys-Overland the world's second-largest automaker, Ford holding the premier position.

In that same year, the American company moved into the Canadian market by purchasing the Weston Road factory of the Russell Motor Car Company. The Canadian company retained a one-third ownership in the new firm, which would be known as Willys-Overland of Canada Ltd. While a few Willys-Overland products were built that first year in the new Canadian plant, it wasn't long before the entire facility was turned over to the war effort, especially to the production of much-needed airplane engines.

Just months after the war ended, the new Overland 4 started rolling off the Canadian assembly line. Seven years later an entirely new series of automobiles was introduced that included the extremely popular Whippet Four and the less successful Whippet Six. In 1926 the Canadian plant also began producing the Willys-Knight, noted for its revolutionary sleeve-valve engine.

The company was hit hard by the Great Depression; sales of its vehicles in both Canada and the United States slumped badly. As a result, at the end of 1933 production of automobiles at the Canadian facility was terminated, though the sale of imported Willys products continued. The next year, company headquarters moved from west Toronto to Windsor, Ontario.

To complete the story, the Willys organization was taken over by American industrialist Henry Kaiser in 1953 and renamed Kaiser Jeep of Canada. Kaiser Jeep was itself taken over by American Motors in 1970.

Willys-Overland Sales Company showroom, Bay Street at Breadalbane, March 11, 1926.

J. Boyd, SC 266-7291

Messrs H.B. Moore and J.H. Hughes opened their Dodge Brothers auto and Graham Brothers truck dealership on the east side of Bay Street in the latter part of the 1920s. Several years later Arnold O'Donnell and W.A. Mackie purchased the business and began offering Studebaker, Rockne, Hupmobile, Cord, Dusenberg, and Auburn models for sale. Later in the decade O'Donnell-Mackie Ltd. switched to Ford products.

As the roaring twenties turned into the dirty thirties, this part of Bay Street quickly became auto dealer row. The McLaughlin Motor Car Company and Willys-Overland Sales Company Ltd. opened across the street from Moore and Hughes, and Reo Motor Sales moved in next door. National Motors opened a showroom up the street at 941 Bay.

In this photograph (facing page) we see a collection of used cars for sale on the Moore and Hughes lot, some of them the very popular Dodge Brothers model. Mechanics John and Horace Dodge first got into the automotive business in 1902 by building transmissions and supplying them to the Olds Motor Works for their Oldsmobile automobiles. Eleven years later, in 1913, the brothers were supplying engines, transmissions, and axles for Henry Ford's Model T. John was also vice-president of the Ford Motor Company and with his brother held $25 million of Ford stock.

In that same year John and Horace Dodge decided to build their own motor cars. They erected a new factory adjacent to their existing Detroit plant and in 1914 began turning out Dodge Brothers automobiles. In their first full year of production, they manufactured approximately 45,000 autos, putting them in third place behind Ford and Willys-Overland.

In 1917 Dodge Brothers (Canada) Ltd. was established, and four years later Dodge Brothers automobiles were being imported into Canada via Windsor. In March 1924 the company began assembling these automobiles, as well as Graham Brothers trucks, in a former aircraft-manufacturing factory at 1244 Dufferin Street, a site now occupied by the Galeria shopping centre.

Both Dodge brothers died in 1920, and five years later their widows sold the successful auto company to bankers who in turn sold the enterprise, including the entire Toronto operation, to Walter Chrysler in the spring of 1928.

Assembly of Dodge Brothers four- and six-cylinder models continued at the Dufferin Street factory throughout 1928 but was phased out the following year, and production was subsequently moved to Windsor. The "Brothers" part of the name was dropped in 1933.

Moore and Hughes Ltd.,
1009–1027 Bay Street, 1927.

J. Boyd, SC 266-10768

A direct result of the ever-increasing number of vehicles on city streets was an extensive program of street widenings and extensions, as well as the realignment of such major intersections as College/Carlton/Yonge. Originally College and Carlton did not meet at Yonge but in fact intersected Yonge at separate locations, the College/Yonge intersection being approximately 210 metres further north than the one at Carlton/Yonge.

In a report prepared in 1911, the Civic Improvement Committee recommended that steps be taken to eliminate this kink in what was becoming a very congested part of town. East-west traffic on both College and Carlton was forced to turn south or north (depending on which street they were on) at Yonge, travel a short distance, then jog again to continue the journey. However, no action was taken.

In 1929 a report prepared by the Advisory City Planning Commission proposed that the jog at College/Carlton/Yonge be eliminated and that Carlton be widened as far east as Jarvis Street. In addition to the need to improve traffic flow in the area, the new Eaton project for the southwest corner of the intersection dictated that something be done.

One of the businesses to suffer as a result of the realignment of the intersection was the motorcycle shop of Herb Kipp. His store and in fact all the structures seen in the photograph (below, left) were demolished to make way for the new street.

In 1911 druggist Herbert M. Kipp, together with Frank Lemon, opened his first motorcycle shop, locating it next to his drugstore at 168 McCaul Street. Kipp moved the motorcycle business to 447 Yonge, just north of Carlton, in 1917 and operated from there until his death in 1930, about the time this photo was taken. Frank Lemon and Herb Kipp carried the famous Indian motorcycle.

More than 5,000 spectators attended the motorcycle hill-climbing competition in High Park, an event organized by the Toronto Motorcycle Club. Several of the winners were well-known local dealers, including Herb Kipp on a seven-horsepower Indian, Percy McBride on a seven-horsepower Henderson, and Wilfred Morrison on a Harley Davidson.

Motorcycle hill-climbing competition, High Park, April 10, 1914.

A. Goss, SC 231-1135

Motorcycle races at the CNE grandstand, 1911.

Wm. James, SC 244-267

Virtually every aspect of the way people worked was affected by the motor vehicle. As well, public transportation improvements changed the way Torontonians got to work. The less reliable horse was phased out during this period (though not completely), as businesses, large and small, adopted the motor vehicle.

City Dairy, milk wagon No. 2, and driver William King Baker, c. 1895.
SC 198-3

City Dairy, advertisement from J.E. Middleton's Toronto's 100 Years, published in 1934.
Mike Filey Collection

The City Dairy was established in 1900 by Walter Massey, the third son of industrialist Hart Massey. Walter had become president of the Massey Manufacturing Company upon his father's death in 1896. The following year, he began development of Dentonia Park, a model farm located on 240 acres of rolling land in the township of Scarborough, just north of the present-day Danforth Avenue/Victoria Park intersection. The name Dentonia was adapted from his wife Susan's maiden name, Denton.

Various agricultural experiments were carried out at the farm, including a revolutionary new process for sanitizing milk.

Up to this time the citizens of Toronto had obtained their milk by dipping their own containers into huge uncovered tanks strapped to the back of wagons that cruised dusty city streets.

As means of marketing this and other revolutionary Dentonia Farm products, Massey established the City Dairy retail store and factory, complete with water tank in the shape of a huge milk bottle, on the east side of Spadina Crescent just north of College Street. City Dairy was eventually purchased by the Borden Company.

Ice wagon,
January 22, 1924.
J. Boyd, SC 266-1881

Located on the south side of King Street, opposite St. James' Cathedral, Gallagher & Company, a popular provisioner, claimed to have been the first Toronto grocery store to use a truck for deliveries. The model Gallagher selected was a Cadillac (seen in the photo), built by the Cadillac company in their Detroit, Michigan, factory during the period 1904–1908. Cadillac motor cars, which were introduced in the United States in 1903, were built in Oshawa, Ontario, from 1923 until 1936.

Gallagher & Company's grocery store, 107 King Street East, c. 1907.
A. Galbraith, SC 568-405

In the photo below, two motorized delivery trucks join a line of horse-drawn wagons along the north side of Albert Street, behind City Hall, as Eaton employees prepare for a busy day's work. Less than six years after Timothy Eaton opened his first Toronto store in early December 1869, the enterprising young man was offering customers a local delivery service. Initially, this service was provided by a single wagon driven by 14-year-old William Elder and pulled by a pony named Maggie.

In 1903 the T. Eaton Company instituted a horse and wagon delivery schedule for customers living in suburban Mimico, Victoria Park, Lambton Mills, Richmond Hill, and Cooksville. The company acquired its first motorized delivery wagon in 1911. By 1919 the firm was boasting that, in addition to its fleet of 200 wagons and 310 horses, it had acquired 66 modern motor trucks with capacities ranging from one-third of a ton to one and a half tons. These vehicles were used for furniture delivery and on suburban delivery routes.

At the end of 1936, the decision was made to retire the horses (traditionally chestnut in colour) in favour of the more efficient mechanized vehicles, and the last of the company's 400 to be auctioned off was Ronald, who went for $165.

The Robert Simpson Company, established in 1872 and located across Queen Street from Eaton's store, also offered a horse-drawn wagon delivery service. At first it was the practice of the company to acquire only dapple-grey horses, but when suppliers boosted prices for this particular animal, Simpson's officials became less specific in their selection. By 1916 the company had 200 horses. That number began to dwindle the next year as battery-powered and gasoline trucks were introduced. The last Simpson horse plodded Toronto city streets in 1928.

With the outbreak of the Second World War in 1939, and with the eventual introduction of tire and gasoline rationing, both department stores reinstated horse-drawn delivery equipment. With the end of hostilities in 1945, the horses were put out to pasture once again.

Eaton's Annex, erected in 1912, can be seen in this photograph in the background right. City Hall (now Old City Hall) is to the extreme left.

Albert Street, west of James, February 19, 1913.
A. Goss, SC 231-1267

The motorized taxicab business was the successor to the livery and stable business of 19th-century Toronto. *Landmarks of Toronto*, newspaper publisher John Ross Robertson's six-volume encyclopedia of Toronto history, informs us that the city's first cab driver was Thornton Blackburn, who had emigrated to Toronto from the United States in 1834. He secured employment as a waiter at Osgoode Hall, where he worked for the next three years. In early 1837 Blackburn, determined to better his lot in life, obtained plans for a new-style of horse-drawn vehicle that was just becoming popular in Montreal. He contracted local locksmith and mechanic Paul Bishop to build one of these new so-called cabs (a name adopted from the French *cabriolet*) in the latter's small factory at the corner of Sherbourne and Duke (Adelaide) streets. Before long Blackburn took delivery of the first cab to be built in the young province. The unique vehicle, which was painted yellow and red and called *The City*, could accommodate as many as four passengers, who entered through a door in the back of the box-like affair.

Blackburn enjoyed a monopoly in the cab business until others, recognizing the potential economic rewards of the venture, filled the streets with similar vehicles.

Another early cab driver was Joseph Hazelton, after whom, it is believed, Hazelton Avenue in the Yorkville area of Toronto was named.

The first motorized taxis in Toronto were operated by Berna Motors and Taxicabs, Ltd., whose office was in the Home Life Insurance building at Adelaide and Victoria streets. The company purchased French-built Darracq automobiles and put them into service in the spring of 1909. Customers were asked to reserve their taxi by telephoning Main 6931.

De Luxe Cab Ltd. was established in 1926 and prided itself on offering its customers cars "void of exterior advertising or glaring insignia," with "room for five, all facing front" and "carefully driven by uniformed chauffeurs."

In 1949 De Luxe and nine other cab companies joined together to form today's well-known Diamond Taxi Cab Association.

De Luxe cabs and drivers, c. 1926.
Wm. James, SC 244-1569

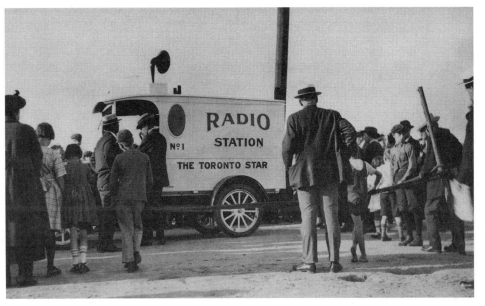

Toronto Star "radio
truck," c. 1922.
Wm. James, SC 244-343

In an effort to introduce radio to as many people as possible, the newspaper developed its own travelling radio station. The unique truck shown here was equipped with a coil aerial, receiving set, special high-power amplifier, something called a magnavox rendor, and a large loudspeaker. All this equipment made it possible for the truck to receive CFCA programs and then broadcast them to the great delight (and awe) of the huge crowds that would invariably gather around it wherever it went.

From 1922 until its licence was allowed to lapse 11 years later (the paper's owner Joe Atkinson was convinced that private radio stations would never succeed as long as the government was involved in the business), the *Star* broadcast a variety of programs – musical recitals, news reports, and sports events, including the first-ever broadcast of a hockey game. On February 9, 1928, CFCA was the first Canadian station to broadcast a church service (from Yorkminster Baptist Church on Yonge Street) and the first to rebroadcast a foreign short-wave program. It was also the first station in the world to broadcast a horse race, from Toronto's own historic Woodbine racetrack.

A fter broadcasting several experimental musical concerts in the spring of 1922 over the Independent Telephone Company's station 9AH, the *Toronto Star*'s own radio station, CFCA, went on the air on June 22, 1922. The first public demonstration of radio broadcasting took place at that year's Canadian National Exhibition.

At first the new station occupied a rather primitive studio located in two small rooms in the Star Building at 18–20 King Street West. Two years later it moved to new quarters on the second floor of a building at the southeast corner of Yonge and St. Clair.

This yard at Dupont Street and Huron Avenue was only one of six coal and fuel yards the Burns Company operated around the city. Established in 1856, the Burns Company was one of the oldest companies in the city, yet one of the first to mechanize its delivery fleet.

Elias Rogers (see ad), who was born near the small community of Newmarket, Ontario, held an interest in several Pennsylvania coal mines. He opened wholesale and retail outlets in Toronto in 1876, where he sold both coal and wood. It wasn't long before Rogers was the city's largest fuel dealer. He had offices and yards at The Esplanade and Princess, The Esplanade and Berkeley, and Niagara and Davis (now Wellington) streets.

Burns Coal Company delivery truck and wagon, June 17, 1927.
J. Boyd, SC 266-10745

Early in the evening of July 20, 1926, several participants at the Brotherhood of St. Andrew's training camp, who ranged in age from 15 to 31, left their summer campsite at Long Point to paddle a large war canoe across Balsam Lake to Coboconk for supplies. At approximately 9 p.m., the canoeists encountered rough water and quickly lost control of the ponderous craft. The canoe suddenly tipped over, throwing the young men into the water. Of the 15 riding in the canoe, 11 were drowned. The four survivors were able to make it to shore and eventually informed authorities of the disaster.

Nine of those who drowned were from Toronto. Of the nine, seven were buried together in a special plot at St. James' Cemetery on Parliament Street following a moving service in St. James' Cathedral. It was one of the largest mass funerals ever held in Toronto.

Hearse owned by R.U. Stone's Funeral Home carries the remains of one of the 11 victims of the Balsam Lake canoe tragedy from St. James' Cathedral to St. James' Cemetery, July 29, 1926.

J. Boyd, SC 266-8396

Looking south on Yonge
Street at Melrose
Avenue, 1917.

A. Goss, SC 231-510

Following their introduction, motorized vehicles did not replace all horse-drawn wagons for many years, and during the Great War horses were once again employed in considerable numbers on the streets of Toronto.

In this photo, the entrance to Lemmon's plumbing and heating shop at 3423 Yonge Street is almost blocked by an avalanche of hay spilled by a passing city-bound freight sleigh with a broken runner. To the right of centre, we see a northbound car of the Toronto and York Radial Railway, Metropolitan Division.

Bus No.4 was one of a quartet of similar vehicles procured by the newly formed Toronto Transportation Commission in 1921 from the Fifth Avenue Coach Company of New York City. Each was equipped with a four-cylinder gasoline engine that could develop 35 horsepower, had solid rubber tires, and could seat 22 passengers inside and 29 more "up top."

These vehicles were bought to operate, temporarily, on the HUMBERSIDE route, which, it was hoped, would soon become a new streetcar line connecting Dundas Street with Runnymede Road via Humberside and High Park avenues and Annette Street.

As it developed, however, TTC track crews were so overwhelmed with the work involved in getting the decrepit system acquired from the Toronto Railway Company into shape that the decision to build the new streetcar route along Humberside Avenue was temporarily, then permanently, shelved.

The TTC's fleet of unique double-deckers, eight in total, saw service on various city routes, including, as in this photo, the FLEET route, that being the original name of the portion of today's Lake Shore Boulevard from Bathurst to Cherry streets.

In this 1929 view, the bus is eastbound and approaching York Street. The coaling tower for the Toronto Terminals Railway heating plant (where steam to heat many downtown buildings, among them the Royal York Hotel, was generated) is in the right background.

Both the coaling tower and the heating plant at the northwest corner of Fleet (Lake Shore) and York streets have recently been demolished.

The Toronto Transportation Commission's new double-deck bus No.4 on Fleet Street, June 8, 1930.

Mike Filey Collection

James family and their Ford, c. 1922.
Wm. James SC, 244-3542

William James & Sons, Photographers, frequently used motorized equipment while pursuing business. Here William James Jr. and brother Joseph are seen on a 1912 Monarch motorcycle.
Wm James, SC 244-3541

Frank James and his Willys-Overland, 1931.
Wm. James, SC 244-3545

City dump at Woodville Avenue (now Indian Grove) near Glenlake Avenue, June 11, 1914.

A. Goss, SC 231-1459

Brothers John, William, and Augustus Mack began building wagons and carriages in a small Brooklyn, New York, garage in 1894. In 1906, after moving to larger facilities in Allentown, Pennsylvania, the boys turned out their first truck. A few years later they tried their collective hands at bus production, and in the mid-1920s the "shock insulated" vehicle shown in this promotional photograph was produced. Unlike most other highway vehicles of the day, this Mack-designed bus used rubber mounts and bushings to help isolate passengers from the bumps and jolts inherent in pioneer intercity highways.

While the demonstration trip in June 1925 was a success, for various reasons (not the least of which was the Great Depression) there would be no scheduled overnight Toronto–Montreal passenger bus service until 1935. The run was introduced that year by Colonial Coach Lines, a forerunner of today's Voyageur Colonial, the largest intercity bus operator in eastern Canada.

A new interurban bus, manufactured by the International Motor Company (later Mack Trucks) of Allentown, Pennsylvania, sits on King Street East, just east of Yonge, prior to a demonstration trip to Montreal on June 3, 1925.

J. Boyd, SC 266-5509

In 19th-century Toronto, ambulance service was provided by both the police department and the city hospitals, the former transporting accident victims and the latter those with infectious diseases. In both cases the ambulance was, of course, horse-drawn. "Mental cases" were referred to the Medical Board of Health, which provided special transportation.

The first motorized vehicle was purchased by the Toronto General Hospital in 1913 with money bequeathed by Agnes Shields. Her endowment also helped build the Shields Emergency Hospital, which still stands on the east side of University Avenue just south of College Street. That first ambulance cost $4,586.10 and could travel, so it was claimed, at the amazing speed of 56 km/h.

The next year, John Craig Eaton (son of department store founder Timothy Eaton) donated a Toronto-built Russell-Knight ambulance to the hospital, with the presentation taking place at that year's motor show.

In 1913 the police obtained their first motor ambulance, and within four years all police ambulances were of the motorized variety. The police went out of the ambulance business in mid-1933, to be replaced by private ambulance companies (usually affiliated with funeral homes), which had made their first appearance in 1905.

Ambulance presented to the Toronto General Hospital by Sir John Eaton, on display at 1914 Toronto Auto Show.

Wm. James, SC 244-57

The Toronto Police Department acquired its first four motorcycles in 1913 and used them to provide a form of traffic control. Fifteen years later, a traffic division was established and began working out of No. 2 Police Station at 75–85 Dundas Street West. The cycles were kept in that station's garage.

For the 1928 portrait seen below, traffic officers, their 19 motorcycles, and Chief Draper (in mufti or plainclothes) gathered on the south side of Dundas, just east of No. 2 Station.

In 1932 the division moved into a new building on Ordnance Street near the CNE Grounds. Today the Metro Toronto Police Department has 128 motorcycles.

Incidentally, the department obtained its first automobile in 1914 (for the use of inspectors) and today has 1,120 vehicles.

Officers of the Toronto Police Department's first traffic division, 1928.
Wm. James, SC 244-1014

Inspector Charles Greenwood, Toronto police motorcycle squad, 1928.

Wm. James, SC 244-1009

Adelaide Street West fire
hall, 1919.
Wm. James, SC 244-11

In 19th-century Toronto, the possibility of fire was a constant concern. In the first part of that century firefighting had been limited to throwing buckets of water on any conflagration. To make sure there were sufficient buckets at hand for this purpose, an ordinance was passed in 1800 requiring that every householder ensure that two buckets capable of holding two gallons of water be available at all times to fight any fire that might break out.

Since fires were frequently caused by overheated chimneys, an amendment was enacted requiring that each householder also keep two ladders, one on the ground level to reach the eaves of the house and a second carefully affixed near the chimney.

Over the years, a variety of hand-propelled, hand-operated "fire engines" were acquired and strategically stored around the little town. All the while, however, the actual firefighters remained strictly a volunteer lot.

In the early 1860s, the first steam pumpers made an appearance, as did the first horses to pull the heavy equipment. Initially, the horses were supplied under contract by various livery owners, but soon the department purchased its own supply.

By the 1870s, the city fathers began to see the wisdom of having a permanent fire department, complete with paid firefighters, to protect the community's 50,000 or so citizens. In 1874 the Toronto Fire Department, with 50 officers and men and a budget of less than $40,000, was established.

The department's 1895 annual report reveals that the force had grown to a total of 115 men working out of 15 fire halls. Their roster of equipment listed 15 wagons and 30 horses, the latter number peaking in 1911 at 114.

It was in that same year, 1911, that the department took delivery of its first piece of motorized equipment, a combination hose and chemical engine that was assigned to No. 8 fire hall at College and Bellevue streets.

From then on, the number of horses began to dwindle as more and more motor vehicles were taken on strength. In the department's 1923 report, 34 trucks were listed and only 22 horses. Manpower, all ranks, stood at 652.

On April 7, 1931, the department's last two horses, Mickey and Prince, were retired.

Horse-drawn steam pumper on Bloor Street at Avenue Road, 1912.

Wm. James, SC 244-10

Royal Mail delivery trucks, 1912.

Wm. James, SC 244-124

The City of Toronto's Streets Department was first established in 1888, with John Jones (of Jones Avenue fame) as the department's first commissioner. In 1905 street-cleaning responsibilities had shifted to the Medical Health Officer, where they remained until the Street Cleaning Department was created in 1913. Sixty years later, the department amalgamated with the Department of Public Works.

From the beginning, the department's many carts, wagons, and the like employed horses, and by 1928 almost 400 equines were on the city roster and, at the busiest times, were assisted by another 200 steeds furnished, under contract, by private owners.

Frequently, horses such as Bess and Ripper of the Street Cleaning Department would take first place in the Toronto Open Air Horse Show Parade held annually on July 1.

The biggest expense associated with maintaining this huge stable of horses was the feed bill, which consisted of charges for oats, hay, straw, bran, salt, and carrots. In addition, a full-time veterinary surgeon was on the payroll, as were six blacksmiths, who were responsible for re-shodding the animals once every month.

About 1930 the total number of horses began to drop as motorized vehicles were increasingly acquired, though it wasn't until 1946 that the city's last 25 horses were sold.

Bess, one of the department's nearly 400 horses, with a four-yard roller-type dump wagon, 1927.
A. Goss, SC 231-1291

Not all of the Street Cleaning Department's new motorized equipment was gasoline-powered. The electric flusher, a rather unique vehicle first purchased in 1913, was powered by electric batteries. Even more interesting is the fact that the power behind the street-flushing action was air pressure. The large 1,000-gallon (4,546-litre) tank was divided into two compartments connected by a valve. The front compartment held some 666 gallons of water, while a second compartment served as an air chamber. As water from a hydrant filled the front compartment, the air in this tank was forced through the valve into the rear air chamber, thereby increasing the air pressure in the rear tank. When the sprinkler heads were opened during street-flushing operations, the increased air pressure created forceful streams of water, but only until the air pressure in the rear tank equalized with the ambient pressure.

An electric flusher, 1913 model, August 30, 1935.
A. Goss, SC 231-1298

In 1841 work commenced on the installation of a privately owned waterworks system to serve the city's 14,000 citizens. This arrangement eventually became unacceptable, and in 1873–74 the service was taken over by the city. The next year saw civic officials recommending the establishment of a totally new, "state-of-the-art" (to use today's jargon) water supply system to satiate the needs of a population that had now grown to nearly 70,000.

Sources such as Bond Lake and Lake Simcoe were discussed and, because of cost, quickly discarded. Lake Ontario was the obvious choice, but an inlet pipe constructed out into the lake was also considered cost prohibitive. Officials settled on a cheaper method. In the simplest terms, water would be collected by infiltration into a large basin excavated near the old Gibraltar Point lighthouse on the Island. From there, water would be piped under the bay to a pumping station at the foot of John Street and then, via a network of underground pipes, to homes and businesses throughout the city.

The filter basins on the Island soon proved inadequate, and in 1881 a wooden pipe was extended out into the lake where water was drawn from a depth of about eight metres.

On several occasions, silt or algae blocked the narrow intake, frequently causing the section of pipe under the bay to fill with air, rise to the surface, and then split open. The system would have to be shut down, and while the Rose Hill Reservoir at Deer Park could provide clean water for a time, water carts often patrolled the streets, offering drinking water to those citizens in need.

Water pipe rupture, Toronto Bay, December 25, 1892.
Mike Filey Collection

Auto Flusher No. 2, 1910. In 1910 this modern auto flusher, the first to be acquired by the city, was introduced. Seven years later, the last horse-drawn flusher was retired from service.
A. Goss, SC 231-1987

Citizens gather around a city-owned water cart following a break in the water supply pipe under Toronto Bay, September 1895.
RG 8 14-3-9

This piece of heavy equipment, described as a "self-propelled, full circle" steam shovel, cost the city $8,665 and was used during the construction of the GERRARD line. Much of this route's right of way, especially the stretch between Coxwell and Main streets, was through untouched countryside, requiring the grading of several deep ravines and the levelling of hills.

To provide citizens in the outer reaches of an ever-expanding city with an uninterrupted supply of clean water, city fathers continually authorized upgrading of the various components of Toronto's massive waterworks system.

In early 1929, three years after initial discussions began, city council approved the expenditure of nearly $1 million on the construction of a new 50-million-gallon (227-million-litre), covered water reservoir to serve the northern section of the city. The reservoir would occupy a large parcel of property at the southeast corner of St. Clair Avenue West and Spadina Road. It was the attempted acquisition of this valuable piece of property from the estate of Sir John Eaton that held up the project for many months. Work finally commenced in the summer of 1929, with a portion of the mammoth facility going on stream less than two years later.

To facilitate the delivery of huge quantities of building materials, special pipes, and huge fittings and valves to the construction site, the Toronto Transportation Commission assisted the city by constructing a spur line into the property from its ST. CLAIR streetcar line.

In this photograph, one of the TTC's construction cars, having backed in from the ST. CLAIR line, is seen making a delivery of material to the site.

Note that there's not a hard hat in sight!

Construction of the new St. Clair Reservoir, St. Clair Avenue West and Spadina Road, September 24, 1929; TTC construction streetcar on trestle.
J. Boyd, SC 266-18036

Throughout the period, city council was constantly approving plans to improve road conditions, upgrade bridges, build underpasses, and create grade separations to accommodate the increase in vehicular traffic.

At the same time, the consolidation and expansion of the public transportation system was an item on every agenda.

In the 1902 photo on the facing page, three city workers are involved in the construction of a brick-lined surface gutter prior to the asphalting of this extremely wide street, which in the 1880s had been surfaced with cedar blocks and cobblestones. Because of its width (40 metres versus the normal 20 or 10 metres), numerous catch basins in the street (rather than off to the side) were necessary to carry off the rain.

In 1902, the year city by-laws were updated to include motor vehicles, workers asphalted more than 8 kilometres of the city's streets. That 8 kilometres, much of it on Spadina, brought the total amount of this type of pavement up to almost 64 kilometres. In that year Toronto could boast 410 kilometres of thoroughfares. In addition to the asphalt streets, the Toronto of 1902 had 78 kilometres of streets covered with cedar blocks, 19 with brick, 8 with gravel, and half a kilometre with wood. The rest were still in their natural muddy state.

Also visible in this photograph is a Toronto Railway Company streetcar operating on the BELT LINE, a route that provided passengers with street railway service on Bloor, Spadina, King, and Sherbourne streets. Together these streets formed a "belt" around downtown Toronto – thereby the name of the line. Initially, equipment was of the horsecar variety. Then, on December 15, 1892, electric service was introduced. The BELT LINE was the third city route to be so converted.

After the TTC took over public transportation responsibilities in the fall of 1921, the BELT LINE continued to operate for two more years. It was finally abandoned in favour of separate lines on Sherbourne and Spadina on June 30, 1923.

The SPADINA streetcar, operated with double-end vehicles with return cross-overs at the Bloor and Fleet (now Lake Shore Boulevard) terminals, continued to operate until October 10, 1948, when it was replaced by buses. On March 10, 1992, however, a new SPADINA light rail transit line was formally approved, and it is anticipated that "streetcars" will return to Spadina in 1997.

Also visible in the photo are Knox College, erected in 1874 and still standing in the centre of Spadina Crescent, and the Broadway Tabernacle, a Methodist house of worship that could accommodate 2,000. Designed by E.J. Lennox, the architect of Old City Hall, the church was dedicated on May 30, 1889. In 1929 the congregation amalgamated with the College Street United Church and abandoned its College and Spadina location. The church was demolished in the 1930s.

A Toronto Railway
Company streetcar on
the BELT LINE, Spadina
Avenue, south of
College, August 10,
1902.

RG 8 14-3-67

Same view, August 1993.

Mike Filey Collection

No. 17 fire hall, Queen Street East at Herbert Street, 1993.

Mike Filey Collection

In the early years of the 20th century, Queen Street in the Beach area of the city was unspoiled by traffic congestion, street signs, or streetlights, a remarkable contrast to the often chaotic scene of today.

For many years prior to the turn of the century, the subject of fire protection was important to those living in this area. So concerned were the residents that in 1891 a volunteer fire company was formed and a small piece of property near Queen Street and Lee Avenue leased. Soon a rudimentary fire hall was erected and furnished with sections of hose and other pieces of fire-fighting equipment.

Five years later, a larger hall was built nearby and the volunteer company given $96 annually to cover expenses. This arrangement was significantly cheaper than the cost of financing a regular city fire company. In 1898 the annual grant was increased to $150.

The city's investment paid real dividends when, on the evening of April 19, 1904, the entire heart of Toronto erupted in flames and the 20 or so members of the Kew Beach Volunteer Fire Company immediately raced along Queen to assist the badly overworked city firefighters in their hour of need.

As the number of permanent Beach residents increased (and the number of temporary summer residences in the form of can-

vas tents decreased) so too did the need for a full-time firefighting brigade. City council finally agreed, and in 1905 work commenced on the construction of No. 17 fire hall at the northwest corner of Queen and Herbert streets.

From the vantage point of the new hall's tower, photographer Micklethwaite was able to obtain this view (facing page) looking east along Queen. The large brick structure to the right is Kew Beach School, which was erected just south of the Queen Street/Kippendavie Avenue intersection in 1899. Increasing enrollments resulted in frequent expansions of the original four-room school. In 1962 the old building was demolished and the present structure erected.

Also visible at the extreme left of the photo is a pair of Toronto Railway Company wooden streetcars on the KING route. This service, which used electric vehicles, began operating from Roncesvalles Avenue into the Beach area in the spring of 1893. In fact, streetcars of the horse-drawn variety had bustled along a dirt path called Queen Street as early as 1889.

The present-day streetcar service came into effect with the opening of the loop on July 2, 1922. Originally serviced by KING cars, the route was realigned and renamed BEACH in 1923 and realigned and renamed again, this time QUEEN, in 1937. At this time the cars ran from NEVILLE loop to PARKSIDE loop out Lake Shore Boulevard; the latter terminus was changed to the present HUMBER loop (via the newly constructed Queensway) in 1957. The numerical 501 terminology went into effect in 1979.

Looking east along Queen Street from No. 17 fire hall at Queen and Herbert streets, c. 1906.

Same view, August 1993.

With the introduction of electric streetcars over the two-year period from August 15, 1892 (when the CHURCH route was electrified), to August 31, 1894 (McCAUL electrified), the limited amount of power available to feed into the overhead supply soon proved insufficient. As a result, the company powerhouse at the southeast corner of Front and Frederick streets (formerly a stable for the steeds pulling the horsecars and now the Young People's Theatre) was repeatedly enlarged. One such expansion, that of 1893, necessitated the construction of a huge chimney; constructed out of 500,000 bricks stacked 60 metres high, it was reported to be the tallest on the continent. It was from this chimney that Frank Micklethwaite obtained this remarkable photo (facing page) of the Toronto of nearly a century ago.

1) Front/West Market intersection
2) North St. Lawrence Market building (demolished)
3) weigh scale (middle of Front Street just east of Jarvis, erected c. 1830, demolished)
4) Jarvis Street
5) building on northeast corner of Front and Jarvis streets, site of Golden Griddle restaurant
6) hay carts parked on Front Street
7) St. James' Cathedral
8) St. Lawrence Hall
9) Royal Hotel, northwest corner of Front and George streets (demolished)
10) Confederation Life Building, northeast corner Richmond and Yonge streets
11) early E.J. Lennox–designed "skyscraper," southeast corner of Jarvis and King streets (demolished)
12) electric streetcars on Front Street
13) Black Horse Hotel, northeast corner of Front and George (demolished)
14) Metropolitan Methodist (now United) Church, northwest corner of Queen and Church streets
15) St. Michael's Cathedral, northwest corner of Church and Shuter streets

View looking northwest from Toronto Railway Company chimney, Frederick Street and The Esplanade, c. 1894.

RG 8 14-1-46a

Ideal Bread Company wagon, Earlscourt district, c. 1912.

Wm. James, SC 244-31

Good health has always been a concern of Torontonians. The editorial cartoon, from the October 19, 1907, Toronto Evening Telegram emphasizes the citizens' outrage with the privately owned street railway company.

Painted pure white, this child's hearse is probably destined for Prospect Cemetery on the north side of St. Clair Avenue just west of Lansdowne. This cemetery, which opened in 1890 on the site of a farm situated well outside the city limits of the day, was still relatively vacant when this sad interment took place. A.W. Miles, one of the city's pioneer undertakers, who operated a funeral parlour at 396 College Street, introduced the concept of motorized hearses during the latter part of the First World War. Some people condemned Miles, believing that rushing the deceased to their final resting place in a motorized hearse was an undignified practice.

A. W. MILES, Undertaker

has introduced for his exclusive use the first and only Motor Hearse for children's funerals in Toronto.

He has also introduced the Motor Ambulances, Hearses, Limousines, and Funeral Chapels.

Offices in London, England, and connections to all parts of the world. *1918*

TORONTO HEAD OFFICE: 396 COLLEGE ST.

Telephones College 2757—
1752

Inset: A.W. Miles's newspaper ad for his new motorized children's hearse, October 18, 1918.
Humphrey Funeral Home, A.W. Miles Chapel

Heavy rain and melting snow turned St. Clair Avenue West into a quagmire in the spring of 1912.
Wm. James, SC 244-39

In the early years of the 20th century, traffic over the Lakeshore Road increased to such a level that safety demanded major improvements. In 1914 the Toronto-Hamilton Highway Commission was established, and work finally started on the massive undertaking in the late fall of that year. Just three days short of a full three years, on November 7, 1917, a new concrete highway was officially opened to traffic.

Described by one commissioner as "the most important section of the most important highway in the country," the new Toronto-Hamilton Highway was void of dangerous curves and all excessive grades had been smoothed out.

A Commer delivery truck, owned by Harpham Brothers, "plows" its way through the mud on the Lakeshore Road, 1914.

Wm. James, SC 244-1119

Morley Avenue, 1912.

Wm. James, SC 244-41

In this photo Bloor Street still has a pioneer look to it, though progress has resulted in the construction of a modern wooden sidewalk on the south side. The street was named for an early Yorkville inhabitant and industrialist, brewer Joseph Bloore (to give his surname the spelling as appears on his gravestone). Indian Road was so named because that's precisely what it was, a pathway through the forest traversed by native people. Tradition states that the modern thoroughfare was laid out on top of that pathway by the warden of High Park, John George Howard.

Bloor Street, looking east at Indian Road, 1913.

A. Goss, SC 231-1808

The first streetcars to appear on Bloor this far west were the three double-end cars of the Toronto Civic Railways, a city-owned street railway system operating five separate lines. The BLOOR WEST line went into service between Dundas Street and Quebec Avenue on February 23, 1915.

Over the years this route was extended westerly, first to Runnymede Road, then, two years after the TTC was formed, to the new JANE loop that opened on the last day of 1923. With the completion of the railway underpasses on Bloor Street between Lansdowne and Dundas in the summer of 1925, the separate BLOOR WEST and BLOOR routes were amalgamated. The resulting BLOOR line operated from Jane Street on the west to Luttrell Avenue on the east. Streetcars on Bloor and the Danforth were finally displaced on February 26, 1966, by the new BLOOR-DANFORTH subway, which, in its initial configuration, operated between Keele Street and Woodbine Avenue.

As the driver carefully navigates his horse and cart down the Walmer Road hill, a shiny new "horseless carriage" takes the hill in easy stride. At the top of the hill we see the stables and carriage house erected in 1906 by Toronto multi-millionaire and omni-present entrepreneur Sir Henry Pellatt. A few years before, Sir Henry had purchased 15 acres of property from James Austin, and work soon began on both the carriage house and stables. Over the following years, the majestic stables not only were home to the knight's champion Percherons and Clydesdales, but also afforded accommodation for several automobiles, including one of the city's first electric cars.

Four years after the carriage house and stables were completed, work commenced on Casa Loma. The Pellatts occupied the castle in the summer of 1913, only to be forced out a decade later by exorbitant heating bills and sky-rocketing property taxes. A completed section of the castle's perimeter wall is visible in this photograph, and stone for the rest of the wall lies on the ground nearby.

Looking north on Walmer Road from Davenport Road, 1913.

A. Goss, SC 231-1778

York Street, looking south to Front Street, 1915. Note the Simpson's electric delivery van proceeding north on York Street across the Front Street intersection and the constable directing traffic at the intersection without the aid of traffic signals or lights.

A. Goss, SC 231-1969

In the 1917 photo on the facing page, steelworkers employed by the Montreal construction firm of P. Lyall and Sons skilfully guide the huge girders that form the skeleton of the Great Hall portion of Toronto's new Union Station into place. Down at street level a Toronto Railway Company streetcar on the BATHURST route rattles by.

Preliminary work on the station began on September 26, 1914, and although wartime activities and shortages slowed progress, the station was ready to go into operation in the fall of 1920. Unfortunately, work on determining the final location of the railway tracks that would serve the $3-million station hadn't progressed as expeditiously.

Another seven years went by before work had progressed sufficiently to permit a pair of royal visitors to officially open the magnificent building, in August 1927. Afterwards, Edward, the Prince of Wales, and his brother Prince George travelled to western Canada for a short stay at Edward's Alberta ranch. They then returned to Toronto to dedicate another of its landmarks, the Princes' Gates.

Also visible in this 1917 photo is a portion of the old Walker House Hotel, protruding into the right side of the view.

Toronto's new Union Station on Front Street under construction, August 1, 1917.

Mike Filey Collection

In this view we see two of the most intriguing transit schemes to ever operate in our city. In the foreground left, the tracks of the privately owned Metropolitan Division of the Toronto and York Radial Railway (T&YRR) are evident. In its earliest version, this system operated as a horsecar line from the city's northern limits (in 1877 still well south of St. Clair Avenue), running north on Yonge and eventually reaching the community of Eglinton in 1885. Over the next few years, the service was elec-

trified (1889) and continuously extended further and further north to serve York Mills (1890), Richmond Hill (1896), Newmarket (1899), and Jackson's Point (1907), reaching its ultimate northern terminus at Sutton on the shores of Lake Simcoe in 1909.

With the establishment of the new municipally owned Toronto Transportation Commission by an act of the provincial government in June 1920, the city portions of the T&YRR's three

Yonge Street, looking north to Balliol Street and the old BELT LINE Railway bridge, 1915.

A. Goss, SC 231-485

lines (the Metropolitan plus the Scarborough and Mimico divisions) were acquired for $585,000, double-tracked, and incorporated into the city streetcar network.

The side-of-the-road tracks in this view were torn up, double tracks laid in the centre of the street, and the YONGE streetcar route extended to the city limits (just north of Glen Echo Road) on November 2, 1922. This streetcar route was shut down when the YONGE subway was opened on March 30, 1954.

The trackage outside the city was also purchased by the city, and this service was operated, under contract, by the Hydro Electric Power Commission of Ontario (now Ontario Hydro). In 1927 the service was turned over to the TTC, which operated it until partial abandonment on March 16, 1930.

After a three-month cessation of service, the Toronto–Richmond Hill section was reactivated. It operated until total discontinuance occurred on October 10, 1948, ostensibly because of electrical power shortages after the war. After more than seven decades of service, streetcars on north Yonge Street disappeared.

The bridge in this photo carried the tracks of another, though much less successful, private transit enterprise, one that stumbled through just 870 days of service. The BELT LINE Railway was the creation of the Belt Land Company, an enterprise run by a group of wealthy Toronto entrepreneurs. After buying up real estate north of the city, this company had initiated a commuter steam railway service to provide transit to and from the city for those who purchased the company's suburban land. The first train on the new BELT LINE'S DON loop entered service on July 30, 1892. Its route followed track east from the old Union Station (then on Front west of York), north up the west side of the Don Valley, through a glen to the unused eastern section of the Mt.

Pleasant Cemetery property, west along the northern edge of the cemetery to Yonge Street, across Yonge on the steel bridge seen in the photo, northwesterly to just east of the intersection of the two concession roads now called Bathurst Street and Eglinton Avenue, westerly once more on the north side of the latter concession road, connecting with the Grand Trunk Railway (just west of Caledonia Road), then south to the waterfront and back to Union Station.

There was also a HUMBER loop that used track west of the station to access a line built on the east bank of the river. This route then curved east to connect with the same Grand Trunk track as that used by the DON loop, and returned to the station.

No sooner had the BELT LINE gone into service than the land boom collapsed. Trains now ran with few, if any, passengers. The BELT LINE was soon taken over by the Grand Trunk Railway, whose equipment and crews had been operating the line since its inception.

The last train to operate under the auspices of the Belt Land Company chugged out of Union Station on November 17, 1894. During the First World War, much of the trackage was removed and shipped overseas to help in the war effort. Other sections simply reverted to freight use.

The route of the old BELT LINE is now undergoing a rebirth, of sorts, as a linear or "walking" park.

In this photo, the driver of the right-hand-drive automobile, stopped at a King Street corner, seems uncertain as to which side of the road he should be on. Perhaps sticking to the middle of the street was his safest bet.

Actually, the choice of driving on the right or left side of the road back at the turn-of-the-century depended on what province you were driving in at the time. For instance, in the Maritime provinces, Newfoundland, and British Columbia, drivers kept to the left, while in Quebec and Ontario and in the Prairie provinces, "keep right" was the rule.

It wasn't until the early 1920s that the latter rule became consistent across the country, except on the "Rock" (Newfoundland, which at that time was not yet part of Canada). Motorists in Newfoundland didn't make the switch until 1947, though one wag suggested that the trucks and buses should try it first and if it worked out, autos would follow.

The tradition of driving on the right in Ontario may be explained in one of two ways: either the custom came to this province from neighbouring Quebec or it started with the settlers arriving from south of the border, most of whom were accustomed to driving their huge Conestoga wagons on the right so that the driver had a clear view of the road ahead.

Some of the prominent buildings in the photo are (left to right), the seventh Toronto Post Office (with massive pillars, erected 1853 and still standing); next to it, the Masonic Hall (1857, demolished); at the top of the street, the eighth Toronto Post Office (1871–73, demolished); and on the east side of the street at number 17, the nicely restored former Consumers' Gas building (1876).

Toronto grew rapidly in the years that followed the end of the Great War, not only in population but in area as well.

Civic officials were hard pressed to provide adequate public transportation to and from the more suburban areas of the city. Their demands that the existing privately owned Toronto Railway Company lay new track and purchase additional vehicles to service these areas fell on deaf ears.

Finally, in an effort to come to grips with the problem, the city established its own municipally controlled system called the Toronto Civic Railways. The railway was given a mandate to provide a transit service for those taxpayers living in the fringe areas of the city.

Soon after the first three Civic routes, GERRARD, ST. CLAIR, and DANFORTH, were built and opened, construction began on the BLOOR WEST line to serve the populace living in the western extremities of the city. By the end of February 1915, a minimal service, between Dundas Street and Quebec Avenue, was up and running along a very rural looking Bloor Street.

Plans to extend this line west to Runnymede Road were stalled because of a huge gaping gully near the present Glendennan Avenue/Bloor Street intersection that effectively blocked the way. Filling in this barrier, to bring the right of way for the Bloor Street extension to grade, took almost three years.

In spite of the difficulties at hand, city crews completed their assigned task, streetcar track was laid down, overhead wires were strung, and service to Runnymede Road commenced on November 12, 1917.

In September of 1921, the municipally owned Toronto Transportation Commission (which had just absorbed both the Toronto Civic Railways and the Toronto Railway Company and was now responsible for all public transportation in the city)

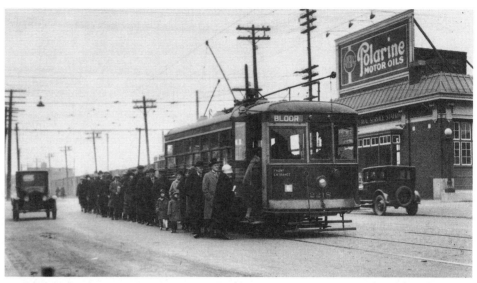

constructed another short extension, taking the BLOOR WEST route to Jane Street. A few months later a loop was installed on the south side of Bloor opposite Jane.

Streetcars continued to provide service on Bloor (and out the Danforth to Luttrell Avenue) until they were superseded on February 26, 1966, by the shiny new silver BLOOR-DANFORTH subway cars.

Note the Imperial Oil service station on the north side of the road and a couple of "flivvers" on a relatively car-free Bloor Street. Note also that the streetcar (a former green Civic car now repainted in the new TTC colours) is of the double-end variety, with two trolley poles permitting the vehicle to change directions without the need of a loop.

Transit riders, many bound for downtown Toronto, board an eastbound Bloor streetcar at the Glendonwynne Road stop, March 25, 1924.

SC 266-2266

The ST. CLAIR route, at a length of almost five kilometres between terminals at Avenue Road and Station Street (west of Caledonia Road) the longest of any Toronto Civic Railway route, was officially opened on August 25, 1913. Exactly eight years and seven days later, the City of Toronto took over operation of all five Civic lines, plus several other privately run street railway services, and made them the responsibility of the newly established Toronto Transportation Commission.

Over succeeding years the terminals of the ST. CLAIR line were constantly changed (west: Caledonia, Townsley loop; east: Avenue Road, Lawton loop, Mt. Pleasant Road). Today the 512 streetcar operates between Keele Street and the ST. CLAIR station on the YONGE subway, tracing much of ST. CLAIR's original 1913 route.

All along the five-kilometre stretch of the ST. CLAIR line there were hills and valleys that required grading to permit a level right of way. One of the most difficult obstacles was to be found just east of Bathurst Street where the formidable Well's Hill ravine, 300 metres wide, crossed St. Clair Avenue.

Initially it was thought that the tracks could be laid on landfill. After thousands of cubic metres of earth had been put in place, a severe slide occurred. Engineers rethought the project and decided on a bridge structure instead.

In the upper-right photo we see the 30-metre-long centre span for the Well's Hill ravine bridge being moved to the construction site.

▲ Workers move a massive bridge girder through snow-covered residential streets to the Well's Hill ravine construction site on St. Clair Avenue, January 23, 1914.

A. Goss, SC 231-1870

ST. CLAIR car crosses Well's Hill ravine on temporary bridge while construction of the main bridge proceeds, 1914. The concrete abutments and 12-metre-long east and west approaches are visible in this photo. Workers await the arrival of the giant centre spans.

A. Goss, SC 231-1907

The bridge's centre span in place, March 13, 1914.

A. Goss, SC 231-1909

From the very beginning, public transportation in and around the city of Toronto had been provided by private operators. That ended, at least for the 512,812 citizens of Toronto, with the establishment of the Toronto Transportation Commission by an act of the provincial government on June 4, 1920.

For the thousands of residents living in those areas abutting but outside the city proper, private operators continued to provide service that became increasingly less satisfactory than that enjoyed by the residents of Toronto. In addition, non-residents working in the city of Toronto had to change cars at the terminal and pay an extra fare to continue their journey to or from the big city.

In November 1924 citizens of York Township saw part of the problem solved when the TTC began operating its streetcars on those portions of the Toronto Suburban Railway Company's ROGERS, OAKWOOD, and LAMBTON routes within township boundaries. One year later, the section of the TSR's popular WESTON ROAD line within the township was also converted to TTC operation, and on November 28, 1925, the commission's modern vehicles entered service between Northlands Avenue and the north end of the town of Weston.

Each of these service improvements were regarded by York Township residents as important enough to necessitate a public ceremony.

On the opening day of WESTON service, both residents and business owners along the route joined the festivities. A huge parade, which included a callithumpian brass band, a band made up of volunteer firemen, and a collection of decorated floats, one of which was brimming with pioneer settlers of the area, proceeded up Weston Road. The happy entourage was led by two policemen on horseback and streetcars full of the ever-present clutch of politicians.

York Township TTC inauguration.

J. Boyd, SC 266-6725

As part of the inauguration of TTC streetcar service on Weston Road, a relic of the early days of public transportation in Toronto, horsecar No. 64, was incorporated in the ceremonial parade. Built in 1879, this historic vehicle is now part of the National Museum of Science and Technology collection in Ottawa. The operator of the horsecar on parade day was James Scott, who joined the Toronto Railway Company, the TTC's predecessor, in 1892, the same year the first electric streetcars appeared on Toronto city streets.

Visible in the right background of this photo is the future site of the Black Creek Drive/Weston Road intersection, as is the CN high-level railway bridge over the Black Creek ravine.

Old Toronto Railway Company horsecar proceeds up the Black Creek Hill on Weston Road, November 28, 1928.

J. Boyd, SC 266-6724

On December 8, 1909, after years of discussion, the railway commissioners of Canada ordered that a total of 13 "at grade" crossings be eliminated through the implementation of the Parkdale Grade Separation project, the most extensive grade separation program ever undertaken in Canada. The project would involve constructing four bridges, to carry vehicles over the tracks, and nine traffic underpasses along the 9.5-kilometre railway right of way between the Canadian Pacific Railway crossing at Strachan Avenue and the suburban community of Mimico. Retaining walls in certain locations would also be required.

In order to handle the ever-increasing number of train and light engine movements (which averaged 162 per 24-hour period), the existing two pairs of tracks would be increased to four, with a maximum grade separation of 0.4 percent in either direction.

Most of the construction work consisted of "cut and fill" operations using two large steam shovels, the first cutting in an easterly direction and the other working westerly from Strachan Avenue.

In this photograph shovel No. 743 is hard at work just east of the foot of Roncesvalles. Topographical conditions west of the Sunnyside area right through to Mimico required that the right of way be built on an elevated viaduct, thus the need for vehicle underpasses from Indian Road west. Work on the $1.8-million project was essentially complete by early 1913.

Same view, 1993.
Mike Filey Collection

Parkdale Grade Separation, Humber Bay shoreline, looking east, near Roncesvalles Avenue, 1910.
A. Goss, SC 231-244

One of the most dangerous railway crossings in the city was the one that crossed Queen Street just west of the old Don River bridge. For many years pedestrians, horse-drawn vehicles, and streetcars had been forced to cross these busy tracks at grade.

In 1909 the Board of Railway Commissioners ordered that this hazardous situation be eliminated by erecting a new high-level bridge over the railway tracks that had now, with three railways – the Canadian Pacific, Canadian Northern, and Grand Trunk – using the tracks, become busier than ever. The timing was right because the old bridge over the river, not having been designed to take the ever-increasing weight of the modern electric streetcars, was quickly becoming a hazard itself.

Work on the project commenced in the fall of 1910. To keep traffic moving across the river, the old bridge (built for $35,000 in 1900) was moved south a few yards and the road diverted. Traffic then used the old structure in its new location while work continued on new bridge approaches (one from the east and two from the west), abutments, piers, and a massive steel structure – all of which was designed to carry traffic high above both the railway corridor and river.

Once the new bridge was in place, crews began reconnecting electrical and telegraph wires (the latter being the only telegraphic connection with eastern Canada), water supply and sewer lines, gas mains, and streetcar tracks.

On October 8, 1911, streetcar traffic began to flow across the new bridge. Toronto Railway Company car No. 922, westbound on the KING route, was the first streetcar to cross the new 400-metre-long structure. Automobiles, trucks, and pedestrians were allowed to use the bridge five days later.

The new structure was built at a cost of $250,000, excluding land acquisition costs and damage claims. Immediately after it opened to traffic, the old bridge was demolished.

In 1962, coincident with the construction of the Don Valley Parkway between the Gardiner Expressway and Bloor Street, the east end of the Queen Street bridge was rebuilt to accommodate the new traffic lanes. The west end and steel truss section were untouched.

An Articulated Light Rail Vehicle crosses the high-level bridge, August 1993.

Mike Filey Collection

Looking west across relocated Queen Street bridge over the Don River, 1911; in the background, the new high-level bridge over the railway tracks is under construction.

A. Goss, SC 231-421

An interesting contrast in street railway characteristics is evident in this Micklethwaite photo. Plodding west along Queen Street and approaching the railway underpass is a horse-car (complete with bobby-helmeted policeman standing on the running board) operated by the two-year-old, privately owned Toronto Railway Company. The TRC began operations in 1891 with one of the terms of the establishing act being that the system had to be fully converted from horsecars to electric cars within three years.

In this view, in addition to the heavily laden horsecar, we can see a stretch of 33-kilogram track recently laid and awaiting the heavier electric vehicles. Less conspicuous is the overhead

electric supply wires. Horsecars were introduced on the new QUEEN route on December 2, 1861, making this the second streetcar route in the city's history, YONGE preceding it by a couple of months. QUEEN cars operated from the St. Lawrence Market to Ossington Avenue (then called Dundas Street) via King, Yonge, and Queen. In 1886 the service was extended west to Roncesvalles and renamed HIGH PARK via QUEEN. In order to comply with the terms of the company's charter, the line was converted to electric operation on March 16, 1893. Judging from the clothing worn by the people in the Micklethwaite photo, it must have been a warm March.

The railway underpass near the Queen/Dufferin intersection, one of many that the railways were ordered to construct throughout the city in an effort to eliminate dangerous grade crossings (made even more dangerous with the advent of the automobile), also has an interesting history. In total, four separate railways crossed Queen Street at this point: the Grand Trunk, the Northern, the Toronto, Grey & Bruce, and the Credit Valley. The town of Parkdale, eager to see the subway built, agreed to pay part of the cost, an amount that reached an expensive (for the town's limited number of taxpayers) total of $20,000. This amount, plus a further amount incurred as a result of damages resulting during construction, was one of the reasons the City of Toronto refused to annex Parkdale following the town's first request in 1885. Annexation was finally effected in 1889.

The present imposing underpass was completed in 1898.

Same view, August 1993. Note Articulated Light Rail Vehicle and new natural gas—powered bus.
Mike Filey Collection

In this photo, taken from the west side of the Humber River, a steady stream of cars heads out of Toronto along the Lakeshore Road towards suburban Etobicoke Township. References to a road in the vicinity of today's Lake Shore Boulevard date back to the early 1800s. A visitor to the mouth of the Credit River in 1827 described the road as "being formed of the trunks of trees laid crosswise, without any coating of earth or stones, and was more abominably jolty than any European imagination can conceive." Another wrote: "A corduroy road should have been included by Dante as the proper highway to Pandemonium, for none can be more decidedly infernal."

The road underwent continual improvement, the constant repairing of pavement, ditches, bridges, etc., being financed by money collected at toll gates. These gates, as well as numerous

others on the roads leading to and from the city, remained in operation well into the 1890s.

In late 1914 work commenced on a new Toronto-Hamilton Highway that was to incorporate much of the old Lakeshore Road in its alignment. The projected thoroughfare would be unique in all of Canada in that its overall width would be 24 feet (7 metres) with a concrete driving surface of 18 feet and paved shoulders of 3 feet; the shoulders would slope to the sides, thereby preventing rain water from accumulating on the surface, where it would present a driving hazard.

More than 1,000 labourers toiled on the $600,000, 64-kilometre project, which was finally completed in the fall of 1917. It is now part of Highway No. 2.

Located to the north of the traffic bridge seen in this photograph is a narrow trestle over which radial streetcars ran, first as far west as Mimico (a small community just west of the Humber River), then to Long Branch, and finally, in 1904, to Port Credit. It was anticipated that the line would eventually reach Hamilton and ultimately Niagara Falls. As it turned out, Port Credit was to remain the end of the line.

In the summer of 1931, the old bridge and trestle were demolished and all vehicular and streetcar traffic began using a new structure. This bridge would collapse during the fury of Hurricane Hazel, which devastated Toronto in mid-October 1954.

The city's population as displayed on the large WELCOME billboard sponsored by the Toronto Convention and Tourist Association (the forerunner of today's Metropolitan Toronto Convention and Visitors Association) is somewhat overstated at 804,349. Civic records indicate a total of only 627,231 on the 1931 assessment roles.

There's no doubt that of all the public works projects undertaken in the early years of this century to help expedite the movement of increasing numbers of cars and trucks, the construction of the monumental Bloor Street Viaduct was the most important and the most expensive.

Until the bridge's opening in 1919, that part of Toronto across the Don Valley and north of Danforth Avenue, as well as properties in neighbouring York Township, was virtually isolated from the rest of the city.

As early as 1880, far-sighted developers and politicians advocated the construction of some sort of bridge across the valley. These requests went unheeded until a referendum on the annual New Year's Day civic election ballot of 1913. The referendum sanctioned its construction by a majority of 9,236 Toronto voters.

Even before the project had been given official approval, numerous designs for the structure were submitted to civic officials. City fathers then decided to hold an international competition. However, none of the submissions was deemed

Two conceptual drawings submitted for Toronto's new Bloor Street Viaduct, 1914. Neither design was accepted.
DPW 10-187; DPW 10-189

appropriate. It was then decreed that the viaduct's design would be left to the staff of the city's Public Works Department. In conjunction with Toronto architectural consultant Edmund Burke, the department was responsible for creating the 1.6-kilometre structure that joined Bloor Street with the Danforth and opened up vast stretches of once sparsely inhabited land "over the Don."

The three sections of the viaduct opened at different times, the most difficult, the connecting Bloor section, opening on August 23, 1919. Several weeks later, following a visit to Toronto by the extremely popular Prince of Wales (who, during the visit, sped by car over the new bridge), the $2.5-million structure was renamed the Prince Edward Viaduct.

During the First World War, several innovative military vehicles were developed locally, though much of the war effort went into traditional munitions manufacture, shipbuilding, and the construction of airplanes. However, military vehicles were regularly part of home-front activities and were used to raise patriotic fervour in fund-raising parades and recruiting drives.

Soon after the outbreak of the First World War, several prominent Canadian citizens suggested that a motor machine-gun battery would provide Allied troops with a distinct advantage over the enemy. The problem was finding sufficient money to design and build this new weapon. Thanks to two well-known Canadian financiers, Sir Clifford Sifton and Sir Charles Gordon, an early prototype of an armoured vehicle was developed. Unfortunately, it proved to be less than a total success, and a few months later Sir John Eaton, president of the T. Eaton Company and son of the store's founder, Timothy, donated $100,000 towards the vehicle's further development and subsequent production.

The task was given to Col. W.K. McNaught and the designers and engineers at the Toronto plant of the Russell Motor Car Company on Weston Road. Then, in the spring of 1915, what had become known as the "Eaton Machine Gun Cars" began rolling off the company's assembly lines. In total, 15 were built. Proud Torontonians soon saw the new weapons undergoing testing in sham battles fought in the suburban townships and later that summer at the military camp that had taken over many of the buildings in the Exhibition Grounds.

The new vehicles were heavier than the earlier models, and while not as fast, they were more thoroughly encased in a specially developed armour plate to afford better protection for the driver and crew. One of the greatest improvements, however, was the installation of a revolving turret that permitted the machine gun to sweep a complete circle.

Toronto-built armoured cars at the CNE camp, 1915.

Wm. James, SC 244-857

In the years that followed the successful end of the "war to end all wars," Armistice Day, November 11, was celebrated with a special service of remembrance in front of Toronto City Hall, where a papier-mâché cenotaph had been constructed and covered with wreaths.

Following the 1923 service, Alderman George Shields rec-ommended that a permanent structure be erected in front of the city hall to commemorate the city's war dead. A competition was held, and the design submitted by the local architectural team of Ferguson and Pomphrey was selected.

It was then decided that Field Marshal the Earl Haig, commander-in-chief of the British forces in the Great War, be asked

The Toronto Evening Telegram, January 26, 1916, "On to Victory Campaign" ad.

The Toronto and York County Patriotic Fund Association Charabanc bus, winter 1916. This three-day fund-raising event netted $2,302,829.11.
Wm. James SC 244-952

to lay the cornerstone during his planned visit to the city in the summer of 1925. The invitation was accepted.

Haig arrived at the city's old Union Station (the new station was complete except for the laying of tracks into the concourse) on Friday, July 24, and proceeded in a motorcade to Government House in Chorley Park by way of Front, Bay, Queen, Yonge, Bloor, Sherbourne streets, South Drive, and Glen Road. Along the way, the Earl's car turned into the drive in front of the city hall, where he alighted, listened as a prayer was said, watched the cornerstone descend into place, gave it a tap with a silver trowel, then returned to his car to continue the trip to Government House.

On November 11, 1925, the completed Cenotaph was officially dedicated by Canada's governor general, Lord Byng.

A British tank, nicknamed Britannia, demonstrates its might by crushing a flivver on University Avenue, 1917.
Wm. James, SC 244-733

Motorcade at Toronto City Hall for Cenotaph cornerstone laying, July 24, 1925.
J. Boyd, SC 266-5855

The automobile hadn't been around Toronto very long before the "impact" of its presence was felt on city streets. Fortunately, most accidents were of the fender-bender variety, with the occasional brush with a wayward pedestrian. Then, in 1907, the first pedestrian fatality occurred. Unfortunately, that was just the beginning.

A Toronto Evening Telegram sketch of a 1904 accident.

Aftermath of a collision between a Peter Witt streetcar and runaway rail freight cars, CN Riverdale crossing, Queen Street East, September 11, 1926.
J. Boyd, SC 266-8780

Late in the evening of Saturday, September 11, 1926, thousands were returning home after a full day at the Canadian National Exhibition. Streetcars leaving the Ex were packed with happy but tired Exhibition visitors.

Eastbound BEACH streetcars on Queen Street, each full to capacity, were strung out like beads between Broadview Avenue and the busy Canadian National crossing just east of De Grassi Street. At approximately 11:30 p.m., the crossing gateman rang his warning gong and lowered the gate to permit the safe passage of the International Ltd., rushing its passengers towards the nation's capital. The train quickly passed and the gates went up. The Toronto Transportation Commission's car No. 2412, westbound on Queen and carrying only seven passengers, proceeded across the tracks. Suddenly, out of the inky blackness, four runaway freight cars on the CN line slammed into the streetcar, piercing its steel sides and causing the heavy vehicle to spin 45 degrees before toppling onto two automobiles waiting at the crossing. The most seriously damaged car was saved from total destruction by the crossing gate, which acted as a sort of wedge and thereby prevented the streetcar from totally squashing the auto.

Of the nine people hurt in the bizarre incident, the most seriously injured were the four occupants of the flimsy autos. Two of these required hospital treatment, while the other two, as well as three of the streetcar passengers, received only minor bruises.

If the runaway had hit one of the packed eastbound streetcars, there is little doubt the death toll would have been substantial.

This was the same level crossing where, in the early evening of November 17, 1904, two passengers and the conductor of a

CN overpass as it looks today, 1993.
Mike Filey Collection

wooden streetcar were killed when their vehicle was rammed by a freight train (see inset, facing page).

Though there was talk of constructing a railway overpass following the 1904 tragedy, nothing was done. However, on a day not long after the 1926 accident, TTC crews appeared on the scene to start preliminary work on the building of an overpass. The new (and present) structure opened to traffic on October 3, 1927.

A young couple was returning to their respective homes on St. George Street after a brief late-afternoon drive around town when their vehicle, described in the newspaper as a couplet, skidded on a patch of ice, was clipped by the front fender of a passing streetcar, and was thrown into the path of a westbound streetcar.

Both occupants were taken into a nearby doctor's office. The driver wasn't seriously hurt and after some minor treatment was sent home. Unfortunately, his companion was more seriously injured. She was immediately sent to Grace Hospital for observation but died a few hours later.

Automobile accident on Bloor Street West, March 4, 1918.

A. Goss, SC 231-258

When the viaduct first opened, streetlighting on the bridge was provided by a series of lampposts located in the centre of the roadway. A recently returned Great War veteran was driving east across the bridge with his wife, daughter, and two Pomeranian dogs. As he attempted to turn north at Cambridge Avenue, his car was struck by an eastbound BLOOR streetcar and shoved into one of the light standards. Fortunately for all concerned, while the car was a write-off, none of its occupants was seriously hurt.

A close call on the Prince Edward (Bloor Street) Viaduct, April 6, 1924.

J. Boyd, SC 266-2336

Mishaps on the city streets didn't just happen to motorized vehicles. One afternoon in the fall of 1914, this delivery wagon, loaded with more than three tons of coal, suddenly crashed through the pavement on Margueretta Street just north of College.

A broken underground sewer had washed away the sand supporting the pavement, and when the heavy rig passed over this spot, a seven-by-five-metre hole opened up and in toppled the rig. The driver and one horse survived unharmed. A second horse died.

A loaded coal delivery wagon, its driver, and its team of horses almost disappear when a city street gives way under them, October 9, 1912.

A. Goss, SC 231-1290

Great changes were taking place on Toronto's city streets thanks to the arrival of motor vehicles. Paved streets, service stations, automatic traffic lights, and new car showrooms all reflected the community's growing commitment to automobiles, trucks, streetcars, and buses.

At the same time, new transportation technology on the water, in the air, and on the rails was seen around the city. Often experimental, these innovations also captured the attention of Torontonians. For example, during the hectic period of the First World War, Thor Shipbuilding and its successor, Dominion Shipbuilding and Repair, fabricated a total of 18 freighters and several trawlers at their yard located on the water's edge just west of the foot of Spadina Avenue.

At the east end of Toronto Harbour, the Toronto Shipbuilding Company was also busy in the early years of the 20th century, fabricating large wooden vessels such as the *War Ontario* and *War Toronto*.

Near the foot of Bathurst Street, the Canadian Shipbuilding Company, a shipyard that was in business for a short four years (1904–1908), turned out several large vessels, one of which, the S.S. *Cayuga*, was to become the most popular and longest-lasting Lake Ontario passenger vessel.

The Canadian Shipbuilding Company had evolved from an earlier Toronto shipyard, that of brothers George and John Bertram. As the major creditors of the financially troubled Doty shipbuilding company (which had built the Toronto Island ferries *Mayflower* and *Primrose* in 1890), the Bertram Engine Works acquired the Doty concern in the mid-1890s and soon began turning out vessels such as the Royal Canadian Yacht Club's recently restored *Hiawatha* (1895) and the Lake Ontario passenger ships *Garden City* (1892), *Corona* (1896), *Toronto* (1899), and *Kingston* (1901).

One of the most interesting of all the Toronto shipbuilding concerns was that of Polson Iron Works, a company that opened a sprawling yard on the Toronto waterfront at the foot of Sherbourne Street in the early 1880s.

Over the succeeding years Polson built dozens of vessels. Two of them can still be seen on Toronto Bay, the restored Island ferry *Trillium* (1910) and the Royal Canadian Yacht Club's *Kwasind* (1912).

The *Cayuga* was originally built for the Richelieu and Ontario Steamship Company and was launched on March 3, 1906. Following the merger of several steamship companies in 1913, it became part of the newly formed Canada Steamship Lines fleet. This popular passenger vessel was removed from service on September 4, 1957, and scrapped four years later.

Lake Ontario passenger steamer Cayuga departs Toronto for Niagara-on-the-Lake and Queenston, c. 1920.

A. Goss, SC 231-455

The Lake Ontario passenger steamer *Kingston* was built at the Bathurst Street yard of Bertram Iron Works in 1901 for the Richelieu & Ontario Navigation Company. The ship was later operated by Canada Steamship Lines when the latter took over the R & O and a trio of other passenger steamship companies in 1913. The 8.5-metre-long sidewheeler, with its 273-horsepower steam engine, had a passenger capacity of 855 and operated on the Toronto–Rochester–Prescott route. Her passenger service days were numbered following the horrendous *Noronic* fire that took 119 lives in September 1949. The *Kingston* was scrapped soon thereafter.

In the background of the photograph we can see the new Toronto Harbour Commission building under construction on the edge of Toronto Bay. Its site was intended to demonstrate the commissioners' unyielding faith in the future of the harbour. Prior to the establishment of the THC in 1912, development of the city's sprawling waterfront was virtually out of control. While there had been several attempts to bring some order out of this chaos, it wasn't until the passage of the Toronto Harbour Commissioners Act on May 9, 1911, followed a year and a half later by city council's approval of a clear plan for controlled and systematic development, that the waterfront as it appears today began to evolve.

One aspect of this waterfront development plan was the construction of a new head office for the harbour commissioners, who, with their staff, had been working out of a small office building at the northwest corner of Bay and Front streets. It was decided that the location of the new building would be right on the edge of the bay just west of the foot of Bay Street. The commissioners selected Toronto architect Alfred Chapman's design and work got under way in the fall of 1916. Two years later, the $245,000 structure, with its sparkling exterior of Indiana limestone, was ready for occupancy.

In the mid-1970s the building, now sitting "high and dry," remote from the waters of Toronto Bay as a result of massive landfilling operations, underwent a $2-million renovation.

S.S. Kingston, as seen from the York Street railway crossing, 1917. In the background, the THC building is under construction.

Mike Filey Collection

Of all the ships built at the Polson Shipyard, or at any Toronto shipyard for that matter, by far the most bizarre was the ill-fated Roller Boat of Frederick Knapp, a Prescott, Ontario, inventor. This craft resembled a huge 33-metre-long, 7-metre-diameter rolling pin that was designed to roll over the waves. Passengers and/or freight would occupy a special compartment within the vessel that was attached, in a squirrel cage–like fashion, to the outer structure in such a manner that it would remain relatively level regardless of sea conditions. The craft was launched on September 8, 1897, and was soon undergoing trials. Unfortunately, the Roller Boat never fulfilled the inventor's dreams and was eventually relegated to landfill.

The Polson Iron Works at Sherbourne Street and The Esplanade, c. 1906. Note the remains of Knapp's Roller Boat rusting away at the extreme right of the photo.

A. Goss, SC 231-316.

Knapp Roller Boat at Polson Iron Works, 1897.

Wm. James, SC 244-251

In the summer of 1918, a Flax Harvest Festival, held to raise money for the Canadian Red Cross, took place on the Wallace farm, which was located on the west side of Yonge Street not far north of the new North York Centre for the Performing Arts. Just three months later, the war that had started in the summer of 1914 (and was supposed to be over before Christmas of that year) ended.

Canadian production of the popular Curtis Jenny biplane, an American-designed trainer, started in the Strachan Avenue factory of Canadian Aeroplanes Ltd. in late 1916 but was moved to the company's new Dufferin Street plant early the next year. When production of the JN4 ceased in the spring of 1918, an amazing 1,200 Jennys had been built in Toronto.

The aircraft shown in the photograph was probably based at the Royal Flying Corps training facility situated at the nearby Armour Heights airfield. The site of that 180-acre pioneer Toronto airport is now occupied by the Highway 401/Avenue Road interchange.

A Toronto-built Curtis JN4 soars overhead at the first Flax Harvest Festival ever held in Canada, in Willowdale, August 10, 1918.

Wm. James, SC 244-4556

In this age of supersonic passenger planes and space shuttle flights, the significance of the R-100's visit to Toronto more than 60 years ago is difficult to comprehend. In the roaring twenties the concept of a commercial airship service intrigued the British government – so much so that to encourage its implementation it authorized the construction of two rigid dirigibles, the R-100 and R-101. The former craft was to be approximately 210 metres in length with a maximum diameter of 40 metres and fitted with 15 gas bags containing more than 140,000 cubic metres of hydrogen. It was to be powered by a dozen Rolls-Royce 12-cylinder aircraft engines, giving the craft a maximum speed of 130 km/h. The huge airship, with a carrying capacity of an even hundred passengers, was designed by

Barnes Neville Wallis (who, in this pre-computer era, hired N.S. Norway, better known as Neville Shute, the author, as his chief calculator) and built at a contracted price of £300,000 by the Airship Guarantee Company at their Howden, East Yorkshire, factory. The R-100 took its maiden flight on December 16, 1929.

To promote regular airship service between member nations of the British Commonwealth, an Imperial Conference was convened in London, England, in October 1926. At that meeting Canada agreed to participate in a transatlantic demonstration, and it was decided that the airship earmarked for the prestigious London–Egypt route, the gleaming new R-100, would be used.

First though, a site for the mandatory mooring mast had to be found. After investigating possible sites in Ottawa, Toronto (at the Jail Farm north of the city), and Montreal, experts decided that a location at St. Hubert, Quebec, would be the most satisfactory. By March 1930 the world's most modern airship mooring mast was ready for the huge airship.

The R-100 departed for Canada on July 29. Seventy-eight hours, 49 minutes, and 5,382 nautical kilometres later, the craft pressed its nose to the St. Hubert mast. The locking mechanism worked perfectly, and at exactly 5:37 a.m., Friday, August 1, 1930, R-100 officially arrived in Canada.

Ten days later, at precisely 6:17 p.m., Sunday, August 10, the airship rose majestically from the mast and set a course for the nation's capital. On the lengthy agenda after this flight was a trip over Toronto and Niagara Falls.

As the R-100 headed south from Ottawa, it became apparent that its timing was a little off, and when the airship arrived over the provincial capital most of its citizens were still in bed.

The British airship R-100 approaches Toronto from the lake, August 11, 1930.

A. Goss, SC 231-1139

No problem. R-100 simply made a couple of leisurely circuits of the Falls and "Golden Horseshoe" communities, then returned to Toronto, where photographs pinpoint her passage over City Hall (a huge WELCOME sign had been painted on the driveway) at exactly 9:18 a.m. Thousands of people gathered on rooftops, in the parks, and along the waterfront to catch a glimpse of what the *Toronto Telegram* newspaper referred to as "the silver ghost." It was a sight that would not soon be forgotten.

Later that day the airship returned to St. Hubert, where plans were already under way for the R-100's departure for England the following day.

As successful as the airship's Canadian visit was, it was all for nothing. On October 4, 1930, the second British airship, the R-101, left on a trip to India. The next day it smashed into a hillside in northern France, killing all but six of the 54 on board. The future of Britain's airship program had been sealed.

I n its early days the Toronto Industrial Exhibition, later the Canadian National Exhibition, took pride in presenting the latest technological marvels in the field of transportation. At the 1922 edition of the fair, Redout Jennings Ltd. of Montreal put its newly designed railcar on display. Unlike the hundreds of coal-fired steam engines then being used by the railways, this Canadian innovation was powered by an ordinary six-cylinder gasoline engine developed by the Reo Motor Company.

Gasoline-powered locomotive on display at the Canadian National Exhibition, September 3, 1922.
SC 548-17652

In 1908 the Canadian National Exhibition opened a new structure at the west end of the grounds dedicated to the future of the railway transportation industry in Canada. Called the Railways Building, it featured three distinct (though interconnected) exhibit halls, each devoted to one of the nation's three operational railways: the Canadian Pacific, Grand Trunk, and Canadian Northern. (The latter two eventually became part of the Canadian National Railways system, created by the federal government in 1919.) Within these halls, each company promoted its services and routes through the use of landscape models, photographs, and paintings.

When no longer required by the railways, the building became home to a variety of displays – Vetiscope and Ontario Hydro's St. Lawrence Seaway project to name just two. It subsequently became the Music Building, and then, in 1987, it was almost destroyed by fire. Today, following major restoration work, the building serves as the Seniors' Pavilion and as the site of various displays on the Ex's fascinating past presented by the CNE's Archives Department.

In 1920 officials of the newly established Canadian National Railways began studying the possibility of replacing coal-fired steam locomotives with an engine powered by some other fuel. Coal was proving to be a problem for the operators, as most of it had to be imported and was therefore subject to uncontrollable and steadily rising costs.

Following discussions with engineers in England, Scotland, and Germany, it was determined that a locomotive powered by a combination of oil and electricity seemed to have the potential to replace the coal-powered engine.

Rather than burning coal to generate steam, CN's new locomotive would use diesel fuel oil to power a pair of 12-cylinder engines, each cylinder having a 12-inch (30.4-centimetre) bore and stroke. The power so developed (rated at 1,300 hp at 800 rpm for each engine) would first be converted into electrical energy by a generator and then transmitted to traction motors geared to driving axles that were connected to the locomotive's huge driving wheels.

Actual construction of the first of this new type of locomotive began in 1926 at the Kingston, Ontario, plant of the Canadian Locomotive Company. Trial runs commenced in late 1928 between Kingston, Belleville, Brockville, and Montreal.

On August 26 of the following year, No. 9000 made its initial public appearance, powering the International Ltd. on its busy Montreal–Toronto run. When No. 9000 arrived at the CNE's railway siding, Toronto mayor Sam McBride and Exhibition president Thomas Bradshaw welcomed the visiting dignitaries who had made the trip. These included Montreal mayor Camillien Houde and C.E. Brooks, CN's chief engineer and one of the driving forces behind North America's first diesel-electric locomotive.

Canadian National Railways' revolutionary new oil-electric locomotive No. 9000 arrives at the Canadian National Exhibition station, August 26, 1929.

J. Boyd, SC 266-17668

Photo Identification

1 King Street, looking east from Church Street. St. Lawrence Hall in background. Note wooden sidewalks. (SC 478-33)

2 King Street, looking west to Jarvis Street. St. James' Cathedral in background. (SC 478-30)

3 King Street, looking east to Yonge Street. Fulton, Michie & Company building still stands. (SC 478-19)

4 Queen Street, looking west at Yonge Street. (SC 478-10)

5 Yonge Street, looking north at Queen Street. Eaton Centre now occupies the area on the left side of photo. (SC 478-38)

6 Church Street, looking north at Front Street. (SC 478-36)